WITHDRAWN

THE LIBRARY OF EDUCATIONAL THOUGHT

Edited by C. H. Dobinson

JOHN LOCKE

JOHN LOCKE by Michael Dahl, c. 1696

JOHN LOCKE

Prophet of Common Sense

M. V. C. JEFFREYS

METHUEN & CO LTD
11 NEW FETTER LANE · LONDON EC4

First published 1967 by Methuen & Co Ltd
© *1967 by M. V. C. Jeffreys*
Printed in Great Britain by
Richard Clay (The Chaucer Press), Ltd., Bungay, Suffolk

NOTE ON THE FRONTISPIECE

*Michael Dahl's portrait of John Locke was painted in about
1696, when Locke was 64. Most of Locke's important works
had by then been published. Although his health was failing,
he was still an active member of the Council of Trade,
and was engaged in political and theological controversy.
The portrait shows Locke at the height of his intellectual powers,
and before ill health seriously clouded the last few years of his life.
The portrait is reproduced by permission of the National Portrait Gallery.*

Distributed in the U.S.A. by Barnes & Noble, Inc.

Contents

Introduction

No account of educational thought in the seventeenth century can ignore John Locke, whose *Thoughts on Education* attracted a good deal of attention in his own time, especially abroad, and can be read with enjoyment and profit today. Yet Locke was by no means primarily an authority on education. It is as a philosopher that he won an assured place in the history of human thought. In an age when it was still possible for an intelligent and well-educated man to master many branches of knowledge, Locke was also a qualified physician, and wrote competently on theology and political theory. His book on education originated in letters written to a friend; and Locke is very modest in the claims he makes for it.

Although Locke had little to say about education that was new, and little practical experience of teaching, his book nevertheless has undeniable importance; partly for its effective style, which is vigorous and witty, giving a memorable form to what he says; and even more because he brings to a clear focus the new spirit of empirical enquiry that was destined to revolutionize philosophy and science, and, with them, the theory and practice of education.

No thinker can be properly understood apart from the historical context in which he belongs; for every thinker both reflects the mind of his age and also contributes to the renewal and redirection of that mind. Of John Locke it is especially true that he must be studied in his historical context; for he lived through a very stormy period of history, and was himself constantly involved in public affairs. He was no academic recluse, but an active, sociable person, with many friends at home and abroad, through whom he kept in touch with everything that was going on in science, philosophy, and politics. He was approaching sixty before his books began to appear. No doubt his writing was all the better for the postponement of publication. For, while he gained maturity, he never lost interest in people and things. Though latterly a sick man, he was never a tired or bored man.

One cannot help liking John Locke. And one likes him for himself. His writing is stamped with his personality; and, as one reads him, one comes to know him, not as a remote figure across three centuries but as someone with whom one would enjoy talking, and who would enjoy hearing of some of the things that had been happening since his time. It would be interesting and salutary to have the light of his practical common sense on some of our own problems – on the affluence of teenagers, for example, or the academic rat-race, or the doctrinaire egalitarianism that has confused the debate on comprehensive schools.

The purpose of this study of Locke is to present his ideas about education, both in their historical context, and also in relation to the problems of our own world. This book is in three parts. Part I gives a short life of Locke, and a review of the seventeenth century in England, with particular reference to the thirty years after the Restoration of the Monarchy – the most important period in Locke's life. Part II is an examination of Locke's philosophy, with special reference to his ideas about education, and a brief sketch of educational thought and practice in England during the century before him. Part III is an analysis of Locke's *Thoughts on Education*, pieced together mainly by means of quotation, re-arranged in what I hope is a clear plan. Locke's own arrangement is confusing, often repetitive, as one might expect of a series of personal letters written over some time. In order to put together his views on a particular topic, one often has to gather remarks from different parts of his book. In re-arranging the essence of what he has to say, I have, of course, kept Locke's own paragraph-references, so that comparison with a complete text can easily be made.

PART ONE

John Locke and His World

It is one of the paradoxes of history that the people of the past speak more clearly to us at the present day if we understand them in the context of their own time.

The purpose of the following three chapters is to sketch the main character and problems of the seventeenth century in England, with special reference to the most important years of Locke's active life, and then to give, in that setting, a short biography of him.

1 · The Seventeenth Century in England

The time of the Stuarts and the Commonwealth was perhaps the most turbulent century in English history. It was an age of revolution, of destruction and reconstruction, not only political but in other fields as well – economic, religious, intellectual. In some ways it was like our own age – an age of shifting values and changing horizons. The problems of those times were not our problems; but they are recognizably related to our problems.

In *politics*, Parliament, which had learnt its strength under the Tudors, came to breaking-point with the exaggerated notions of royal authority cherished by Charles I, and the two sides went to war. The Commonwealth ended in an intolerable military despotism, and the death of Oliver Cromwell removed the only man who could have held any kind of republican government together. Monarchy and established church came back in 1660, but with Parliament as an integral organ of government; and a second period of stress and turmoil, plot and counterplot, ended in the flight of James II and the revolution of 1688, when William of Orange accepted the throne of England on terms laid down by Parliament, which have never since been radically challenged.

The political problem of the seventeenth century was the vindication of constitutional government and the rule of law. Without the firm establishment of constitutional government, democracy as we understand it could never have grown in this country and spread overseas. But no blessings are unmixed. It is one of the ironies of history that the hard-won triumph of democracy has brought us not only the inestimable benefit of a great system of social services but also the danger that the will of the individual may be sapped by the securities of the welfare state, and personal responsibility be submerged in the anaesthesia of total provision from the cradle to the grave.

Economically, the problem of the seventeenth century was the swing of emphasis from land to industry and commerce as the main source of national wealth. The Elizabethan voyages had opened up our ocean trade routes and begun to plant colonies. Our seaports prospered, and so did our merchants. The wars with Spain, and later with the Dutch, established the power of Britain on the sea. England became a nation of shopkeepers.

Without that growth of industry and commerce, this country could not have led the world in the industrial revolution, and in the quality of our science and technology. It is another of the ironies of history that this remarkable material progress has brought us the embarrassment of over-population, the uneasy condition of depending for our existence on imported food, fuel, and raw materials, with skilled manufactures (above all, machinery) as our main export, and finally, the danger of being beaten at the technological game by countries which entered the race after us.

In the field of *religion*, the Elizabethan church settlement, for all its pragmatic sagacity, could not permanently quell the eruptive forces of religious zeal. For a time militant puritanism triumphed. Then, after 1660, there was a period of confused and complicated struggle between the dissenters, the High and Broad parties in the established church, and the Roman Catholic influence of the Court. The problem was to put an end to the persecution of men and women for their faith, and to lay down a workable basis of civil equality for members of the different churches. With the revolution of 1688, the established church and the Protestant dissenters came to terms. And, although the Roman Catholics remained deprived of civil rights until 1829, the religious atmosphere of the eighteenth century was so different from that of the sixteenth that it is hard to realize that only one century lay between them.

Without the broad toleration that came after 1688, what we mean today by the basic human rights of freedom of thought could never have come – at least not without violence and bloodshed. The irony of this chapter of history is that, whereas in 1688 almost everyone accepted the truth of Christianity as such, and toleration meant acknowledging the faith held in common by the different churches, today freedom of thought has eroded the foundations of religious belief itself, so that the remnants of the denominations draw together, as minorities do, in self-defence against an increasingly secular world.

In the field of *intellectual speculation*, the thought of Descartes and the work of the Royal Society affirmed the empirical method of modern science which was destined to bring new life to philosophy, mummified in the Aristotelian tradition, and to dispel the dense fog of popular superstition. The problem of John Locke and his friends in the Royal Society (such as Newton, Sydenham, and Boyle) was to establish on a lasting foundation the habitual attitude to thought and knowledge which we know as the scientific method. They did this in one of the most stormy periods of our history.

Without the pioneer work of those men of the seventeenth century, modern science and our modern technological civilization would not exist. In this instance, the irony of history is that, owing to the fantastic growth of specialized knowledge, we have lost the coherent unity of Truth which our forefathers took for granted and enjoyed, and we find ourselves hard put to it to heal the breach between the two (or more) cultures.

It is an important fact that these great changes came, in England, comparatively early and comparatively peacefully. The fairly painless emergence of this country into the modern world has brought us many blessings – democracy, prosperity, and freedom. It has also exposed us to the danger of taking these blessings for granted as part of a natural heritage, rather than as precious possessions to be defended and nourished from generation to generation. And it has obscured our understanding of situations in other parts of the world where these things that we take for granted are either bitterly contested or do not exist at all.

2 · From the Restoration to the Revolution – Summary of Events, 1660–89

In a book of this kind, a piece of straight historical narrative may come as a surprise. It is included because, without it, it would be very difficult to convey the flavour of social life and public affairs in which John Locke was involved and which influenced his thinking. A secondary reason is that, without some account of the politics of that time, no picture could be given of that extraordinary character, Anthony Ashley Cooper, Lord Shaftesbury, a diminutive, ugly, intelligent, energetic, and ambitious man, who for sixteen years was Locke's close friend and patron – a friendship from which Locke gained much, and a patronage which finally proved so embarrassing that Locke had to follow Shaftesbury into exile, where a good deal of Locke's writing was done. If Locke and Shaftesbury had not met, Locke's career would have been very different; he would have seen less of the world, would probably have written much less, and certainly would not have developed his thought as fully as he did.

The Civil Wars had many unfortunate social effects. Political integrity degenerated under the influence of war and confiscation of property. The unpredictability of the political future put opportunism at a premium. The squirearchy was largely disorganized. Young royalist squires had spent their youth in exile, often in bad company, or had grown up with grooms and stable boys when their hereditary estates were seized and sold. At the time of the Restoration many of the upper class had little moral resistance and welcomed the Court's fashionable example of extravagance and profligacy.

The middle classes were still uncorrupted, interested in trade, habituated to bible reading and family prayers, and to the puritan Sunday, which became a deep-rooted English institution down to our own day. Many suffered ruin and imprisonment rather than conform to the severe demands of the Clarendon Code. The penalties inflicted on dissenters struck at the merchant class, and through them at national prosperity. Puritanism was still strong in the towns; and the gaols were full of Quakers and Baptists.

The country gentry for the most part conformed to Anglican worship and avoided persecution. The middle-class recruits to the ranks of the squirearchy, who retained the estates that had come into their hands under the Commonwealth, regarded conformity as a small price to pay for keeping their gains. English Catholics only wanted to be left alone. The most important social cleavage was thus between town and country – the nonconformist commercial middle classes and the Anglican, or quasi-anglican, gentry.

To see John Locke in the context of this fevered and violent period of history – a time of cynicism, extravagance, corruption, and immorality – is to understand better his ideas and attitudes – his hatred of religious and political intolerance, and his belief in reason and in reasonableness as the right approach to human problems. Locke was a prophet of reasonableness in a world that could hardly have been more unreasonable.

Charles II was proclaimed king in May of 1660. Charles had offered a general pardon and religious toleration, in return for which the Convention Parliament (consisting of a mixture of Presbyterians and Cavaliers) invited him to accept the crown. The fact that Parliament summoned the king was far more important for the future than the continued belief in divine right held by the king himself and the restored Anglican Church. Parliamentary government was established, and king and Parliament henceforth regarded as inseparable. They might disagree; but neither could get on without the other. Absolutism and republicanism were both dead.

The army, which a dozen years before had been the terror of the country, was paid off and peacefully disbanded, though it was many a long year before the dread of a standing army was laid to rest in the hearts of the English people. The royal power was clipped by keeping the king short of money. The revenue provided was not enough; and therefore the king would have to summon Parliament frequently to ask for supplies, in return for which he would have to listen to their grievances. No means remained by which the king could raise money without consent of Parliament (except from abroad).

The statesman of the Restoration was Edward Hyde, Earl of Clarendon, and Lord Chancellor, who had been faithful to the royal family in exile. A moderate and wise man, he tried to get general support for the restored government. Church and Crown lands, and private Cavalier estates that had been confiscated and sold by the rebel governments, were resumed without compensation. But landed property which cavaliers had themselves sold to pay fines imposed on them were left in the hands of the purchasers. By this means a large number of new men were brought into the ranks of the squirearchy, at the easy price of attending Anglican worship. Many of these men later became supporters of the Whig party.

The Convention Parliament continued until the election, in the spring of 1661, of the 'Cavalier Parliament', so called because it appeared to be enthusiastically royalist. In fact, it was Anglican and squirearchical (it was the basis of the future Tory party) rather than royalist – as later became clear from Parliament's attitude to Catholicism and the king's dependence upon France, and from the fact that it kept the king short of money. Charles kept this parliament, however, for eighteen years.

The first work of the Cavalier Parliament was to settle the fate of the dissenters. The four Acts known as the Clarendon Code were not directly the work of Clarendon, who would have preferred a more moderate line. What in fact happened – in complete disregard of the new king's promise of toleration – was a systematic persecution of Protestant dissenters (together with the proscription of Catholics).

The Corporation Act (1661) excluded from an active share in

town government anyone who did not take the sacrament according to the Church of England. The Act of Uniformity (1662) required all clergy to accept the Anglican Prayer Book; 2,000 Presbyterian ministers were driven to resign. The Conventicle Act (1664) forbade meetings for public worship under forms other than Church of England; prison and transportation were the penalties for those caught in acts of dissenting worship. The Five Mile Act (1665) forbade any minister of religion or schoolmaster who was not by oath an Anglican to come within five miles of a corporate town.

The intention of this legislation was to prevent a revival of the Roundhead party, which had been the backbone of the army. In effect the Clarendon Code went much farther, and subjected to ruin and imprisonment many of the urban middle class on whom the country's prosperity depended. It was not long before the government became alarmed at the extent to which manufacture and commerce suffered as a result. In the long term it is probable that the severity of the Clarendon Code did more to ensure the triumph of toleration than a more moderate policy would have done.

War with the Dutch (1665–7) was the outcome of naval and colonial competition, in the East and West Indies, on the coasts of West Africa and North America. New York and New Jersey had been captured from the Dutch in 1664. At that time war against the Dutch appeared sound policy to English opinion generally, including that of the king. The growth of the navy was fostered. Nevertheless, Parliament's reluctance to grant the king money led to ships being laid up and crews disbanded. At this moment of our weakness a Dutch fleet sailed up the Thames estuary, entered the Medway, bombarded Chatham, and burnt our best ships.

Meanwhile, in 1665 and 1666, calamity struck London, first by a severe outbreak of plague, and then by the fire which raged for five days and destroyed two-thirds of the city. In one of his notebooks Locke records his observations of the Fire of London from Oxford, a distance of some sixty miles.

At this low ebb of the national fortunes and morale, popular feeling rose against the Court, and the smouldering fear of Roman Catholicism came to the surface. The king was (rightly) suspected

B

of being a Catholic at heart; and rumour (falsely) ascribed the Great Fire to Catholic sabotage.

The scapegoat was Clarendon, who was dismissed by the king and took refuge abroad. In the years that followed, Charles allowed no single minister to have the influence that Clarendon had exerted. Instead he appointed a council of five advisers, known as the Cabal (medieval Latin: *cabala*). The Cabal included Anthony Ashley Cooper, later Earl of Shaftesbury and Lord Chancellor, the ablest, though the most imprudent, politician of his time.

Ashley Cooper had originally supported the king in the Civil War. Then, in 1644, he changed over and was on friendly terms with Cromwell. At the time of the Restoration he negotiated with every party, eventually attaching himself to the royalists as being likely to prevail. At the time of his coronation Charles made him Baron Ashley (he was made Earl of Shaftesbury in 1672), and commented on his 'prudent and reasonable advice'. Locke certainly exaggerates when he ascribes to Ashley the main credit for the Restoration. In the debates on the Clarendon Code, Ashley took a very liberal line, opposing this whole body of legislation against dissenters. Clarendon said that Ashley 'spake often, and with great sharpness of wit'. If Ashley had a sincere and enduring conviction, as distinct from considerations of expediency, it was a belief in toleration, and a hatred of despotism. Ashley's motive for espousing the cause of toleration arose mainly from the knowledge that persecution hampered commercial development. Ashley must have influenced Locke considerably in a liberal direction. Their interest in toleration, together with the scientific experiments fostered by Ashley at his London house, were a strong bond between John Locke and this picturesque but unscrupulous adventurer, with whom Locke seemed to have so little in common.

The great power in Europe was France. Spain was now decadent. The multifarious states of Germany were exhausted by the Thirty Years War, as Austria was by her war against the Turks. The only hope of resistance against the threat of France to overrun and dominate Europe was the small, middle-class, Protestant republic of the Netherlands, rich in colonies and commerce, foremost not only in trade but in philosophy (Grotius, Descartes, Spinoza) and the arts (Vermeer, Rembrandt), but vulnerable because much of her small territory lay below sea level.

Louis XIV naturally wanted to crush Holland. The attitude of Britain was important but unpredictable. The fortunes of Europe, and our own destiny, turned upon the relations between these three powers.

In 1668 England, having fought the Dutch in 1665–7, joined with Holland and Sweden to resist France. It is probable that Charles II was party to this triple alliance only in order to raise his bargaining value with Louis XIV. Charles was a master of the art of using, for bargaining purposes, threats that he never intended to carry out. In 1670 he and Louis made the Treaty of Dover, the object of which was to attack and partition the Dutch Republic. There were secret clauses by which Louis undertook to supply Charles with money and troops in order that he should declare himself a Roman Catholic and win back England for Catholicism. In 1672 war was declared on the Dutch. Parliament was not allowed to assemble. In the same year Charles did what he could for the Catholics in England by issuing a Declaration of Indulgence – i.e. proclaiming toleration for all dissenters, Protestant and Catholic alike.

Charles's war against the Dutch, however, cost more than Louis XIV was prepared to give him, and impending bankruptcy forced him to recall Parliament. Shaftesbury devised the plan, to get more money for the Dutch war, of suspending repayment of bankers and capitalists who had advanced money to the government, giving them compensation in the form of accumulated interest. In this way about £1,300,000 was secured for the government. Although Charles was pleased with Ashley's ingenuity, and made him Earl of Shaftesbury and appointed him Lord Chancellor, this financial manoeuvre shook the banks and commercial houses and discredited the government. The following year (1673) Shaftesbury made his famous parliamentary speech in favour of war against the Dutch, on the theme *Delenda est Carthago*. It is said that John Locke stood by him with the script in case he needed prompting. In the same year Parliament retorted to the king's Declaration of Indulgence by passing a Test Act, which required all holders of office under the Crown to take the sacrament according to the rites of the Church of England. Shaftesbury had miscalculated, expecting the king to give in. Instead, Charles prorogued Parliament and dismissed Shaftesbury from the Chancellorship.

A significant consequence of the Test Act was the resignation from the post of Lord Admiral of James, Duke of York, Charles's brother and heir to the throne. The threat of Popery had come a step nearer to the English people. In 1674 Parliament withdrew England from the war against the Dutch. The Cavalier Parliament now saw our relations in a fresh light; war against the Dutch was no longer the old struggle for maritime supremacy, but a plot to destroy the only effective obstacle to the French conquest of Europe. This was a decisive change in British policy. The defeat of Holland would mean that the Rhine delta was in the hands of a great power threatening our own safety. The same crisis had existed in 1588, and would again in 1793, 1914, and 1940.

Meanwhile, as the French armies entered the territory of Holland, a political revolution in that country re-established the Stadtholderate (virtually a monarchy) under William of Orange. The dykes which preserved the land of Holland from the Atlantic Ocean were cut. The sea rushed in and drowned the country, but brought the French troops to a standstill. The Dutch navy held its own against England and France at the same time, while William negotiated a European coalition against Louis XIV.

The next twelve years (to the death of the king) were the most politically confused of Charles II's reign.

Charles realized that he had roused the bitter opposition of Parliament by his pro-French and pro-Catholic policy. He therefore switched round and, for the rest of his reign, sought to ally himself with Anglican–Tory sentiment. It was a difficult and delicate piece of tight-rope walking.

At the same time Louis XIV saw that he could no longer count on active English help in conquering Europe, and therefore worked to keep England neutral by playing king and Parliament off against each other.

Shaftesbury, after his dismissal from the Chancellorship, had a pretty shrewd notion of the king's secret designs, went over into political opposition, and became the leader of the new Whig party, proclaiming himself the champion of toleration and the liberties of the people.

Charles got rid of the Cabal ministers, and took as his chief minister the leader of the Cavalier Parliament, Sir Thomas Osborne, whom he created Earl of Danby. Danby was the first minister to owe his position unequivocally to the prevailing will of the House of Commons. He was the real founder, if not the originator, of the Tory party, as Shaftesbury was of the Whigs.

Danby was in power for four years (1674–8). During that time he opposed France and befriended Holland. He negotiated the marriage of Mary, daughter of James, Duke of York, to William of Orange (who was himself the son of Charles's sister, Mary), and thus secured the Protestant succession to the throne and made it virtually certain that William of Orange would follow James of York on the throne of England. At this time the Tory party were more devoted to the House of Orange, and more hostile to France, even than the opposition leaders.

Meanwhile Shaftesbury got himself more and more deeply involved in political intrigue, including his connexion with the Popish Plot. In and out of office, his career in these years was eventful, unpredictable, and finally disastrous. The king grew increasingly suspicious of Shaftesbury, who was practising the arts of the demagogue with considerable success, spreading rumours of plots against the king's life, of Papist attacks on England, backed by France, and of Papist plans for a second great Fire of London. In 1677 Shaftesbury was imprisoned in the Tower, but released the following year.

Danby was trying to do two things. In the first place he wanted to use Parliament to control the Court and check Roman Catholic influence. Charles adjourned Parliament (1677) when they put pressure on him to help the Dutch against France, but could not manage without the money which only Parliament could supply. For a time Charles was accepting money from Parliament to make war on France, and also from Louis XIV for *not* making war on

France. For his part, Louis XIV was willing to bribe the parliamentary opposition as well as the king, to prevent war. Parliament, in general, was anxious for war against France, but afraid to trust the king with money and troops.

Danby's second aim was to use existing legislation to crush the dissenters, and the newly organized Whig party which drew their support largely from the dissenters. Into this situation the Popish Plot exploded, and gave Shaftesbury irresistible opportunities for intrigue.

The Popish Plot was only to a very limited extent a genuine plot, but was enormously exploited for propaganda purposes. The story of Titus Oates ('a clergyman of the Church of England' who had 'by his disorderly life and heterodox doctrine drawn on himself the censure of his spiritual superiors, had been compelled to quit his benefice, and had ever since led an infamous and vagrant life. He had once professed himself a Roman Catholic, and had passed some time on the Continent in English colleges of the Order of Jesus') provided Lord Macaulay with the subject of one of his vigorous, though not most dispassionate, pieces of historical writing. Oates's stories of a great plot to recapture England for Rome were far from accurate, and became increasingly extravagant. There was, however, a substratum of truth in the evidence provided by the papers of Edward Coleman, who had been private secretary to the Duke of York. Most of Coleman's papers had been burnt, and it did not need much ingenuity to suggest that the material which had been destroyed must have contained more damning evidence than the papers that survived. Shaftesbury and his supporters leapt upon the opportunity, and blew up the 'plot' to enormous dimensions. Shaftesbury managed, as chairman of a committee appointed by the House of Lords, to get into his own hands the issue of warrants for arrest and examination of prisoners. When Parliament met in 1678, the Whigs moved a bill to exclude James of York from the throne. The Tories, on the other hand, proposed only to limit his powers. Louis XIV chose this moment to disclose to the Whigs his secret treaty with King Charles. Shaftesbury piled this new fuel on the fire. There was something like a reign of terror, and numerous quite innocent victims were hunted and imprisoned for alleged complicity in the Plot. Danby himself was threatened with impeachment (largely under pressure from Shaftesbury); Charles saved him from standing trial by dissolving Parliament in January 1679 and putting Danby in the Tower of London.

In April 1679 Charles surprisingly appointed Shaftesbury President of the Council, possibly with the idea of keeping him under his eye and so out of mischief. But Shaftesbury's career was near its end. The struggle over the Exclusion Bill led the king to dissolve Parliament. Shaftesbury was dismissed from office in October 1679. He was out of office until his flight from the country in 1682, soon after which he died abroad. One of his last acts before leaving England was to stage-manage an anti-popish pageant in London, including the burning of the Pope in effigy.

In spite of his fatal passion for intrigue, Shaftesbury had statesmanlike ideas ahead of his time. He believed in parliamentary government, toleration (at least for Protestants), and freedom, civil and commercial. He remained true to these beliefs throughout his career. He bequeathed to the Statute Book one vitally important piece of constitutional legislation – the Habeas Corpus Act of 1679, which made it compulsory for the judges to issue, on application, the writ of Habeas Corpus (preventing imprisonment without trial). Thus a rather uncertain common law right became a sure part of the citizen's heritage.

Between 1679 and 1681 there were three successive Parliaments with Whig majorities, which hounded innocent Catholics to death, and (with Shaftesbury's influence again) involved themselves in treasonable negotiation with the Duke of Monmouth (an illegitimate son of Charles II) as a possible heir to the throne in place of James. In 1680 the Exclusion Bill, after several attempts, was passed by the House of Commons by a narrow majority, but thrown out by the Lords.

Shaftesbury and his party had so overplayed their hand that they drove moderate opinion on to the Tory side. The rank and file of the country gentry and high church clergy not only rallied to consolidate the Tory party, but even united with the Court. Charles, who had received fresh supplies of money from Louis XIV, took the Whigs by surprise and put an end to the attempt to pass an Exclusion Bill, by dissolving the third Whig Parliament in 1681.

No Parliament met for the rest of the reign. After the Whig *débâcle*, Tory reaction was unchecked, and dissenters were relentlessly persecuted. Town corporations, including London, were re-modelled to exclude the Whigs (a grosser interference with local liberties than anything the Tudors would have attempted, and only possible by the combination of Court and Tories). By now the Tories were so determined to suppress the dissenters that they were prepared to accept a Catholic heir to the throne and swallow their fears of Roman Catholicism. Conspicuous in its attitude of unconditional surrender to the royal will was the University of Oxford – until James II's blundering lost even that citadel of non-resistance.

The Whig opposition went to pieces. They were divided as to whether to support Monmouth, or William of Orange, or try for a republic. Shaftesbury, driven from one desperate expedient to another, was involved with Monmouth, and also with the Rye House Plot of 1683, an attempt by old Roundhead soldiers to way-lay and murder the king and the Duke of York on their way back from Newmarket races. The plot (June 1683) failed because the king changed his travelling arrangements. Some Whig leaders were arrested and executed. Shaftesbury had already fled the country disguised as a Presbyterian minister and died in Holland (January 1683).

In the last years of his reign Charles had the mastery of English politics by virtue of his extremely skilful handling of a confused situation. He had no armed force at his disposal, and not much money. His victory was a triumph of political manoeuvring, the essence of which was to induce Louis XIV and the Whigs to bid against one another to restrain him from extreme measures which, in any case, he had no intention of adopting. As things turned out, he took money from France. But, had he chosen to summon Parliament, the House of Commons would have been equally ready to supply him.

Charles died in February 1685, leaving his brother to inherit a situation in which the great Tory majority were the ardent champions of Church and Crown, and the Whig opposition was leaderless and discredited. James II proceeded, in a remarkably short space of time, to ruin this strategic position.

Charles's remodelling of the Corporations produced a Tory Parliament (elected in 1685) even more royalist than the Cavalier Parliament of 1661. It voted generous supplies. But it was not prepared to endure the imposition of Roman Catholicism, which was clearly the new king's aim.

The collapse of Monmouth's rebellion in 1685 and the ruthless vengeance taken on the west country puritans who supported him, shocked the public conscience even in those stormy times, and hastened the natural revulsion of feeling against James and Catholicism. No doubt Jeffreys has suffered undeservedly at the hands of Whig historians. He was doing his job honestly according to his lights; and it was at best a dirty job. The important point is that the judiciary was still thought of, and could think of itself, as an instrument of royal policy. And it needed the Revolution of 1688 to establish the political independence and professional integrity of the system of British justice.

The king wanted rebellion smashed and the dissenters destroyed. Jeffreys did the job thoroughly. Three hundred of Monmouth's supporters were executed and 800 banished. By the roadsides in the west country the bodies of victims, soaked in tar, hung from gibbets.

James alarmed and angered Londoners by maintaining an army of 30,000 men camped on Hounslow Heath, officered by Roman Catholics and largely recruited from imported Irish peasants. He claimed to suspend the laws of the land at will. He lost the intense loyalty of Oxford University by turning the Fellows out of Magdalen and converting the College into a Catholic seminary. This stupid act turned the home of lost causes into a hotbed of revolutionary enthusiasm overnight, and the flag of the House of Orange was hoisted in the High.

Events moved fast. Monmouth's collapse brought William of Orange a step nearer the throne of England. All English Whigs and dissenters fixed their hopes upon him. English Catholics for the most part wanted no more than to be allowed to keep their property and live in peace. William was wise enough to promise them toleration in advance.

Meanwhile Louis XIV in 1685 revoked the Edict of Nantes, which had eased the position of French Protestants. No longer protected by the Edict, these Huguenots were fiercely persecuted, tortured, and sent to the galleys. Those who could escaped from France; many came to England and contributed to English industrial enterprise.

The swing of opinion against James's Catholic policy, and the persecution of Protestants in France, hopelessly discredited the Tory doctrine of non-resistance. During James's reign Tories and High Churchmen found themselves excluded from positions of authority in central and local government. James tried to replace them by Catholics, and then in desperation made overtures to the Protestant dissenters. Finally all clergy were commanded to read from their pulpits a royal Declaration of Indulgence, suspending all disabling laws against Catholics and dissenters alike. Seven bishops, including the Archbishop of Canterbury, petitioned against the order. They were sent for trial, and were acquitted by a jury of brave men. That same night (30 June 1688) an invitation was sent by Whig and Tory chiefs to William of Orange. The birth of a Prince of Wales on 10 June had made revolution inevitable, and persuaded the majority of the Tories to put their money on William of Orange. One of the signatories of the letter to William was the Earl of Danby.

The expedition of William of Orange (early November 1688) might not have been easy, because of danger from France. But James II (who, when he did not do the wrong thing, did the right thing at the wrong time) chose this of all moments to repudiate publicly Louis XIV's protection. He then made his unregretted exit from the scene by taking flight to the continent.

With William and Mary, as a member of their entourage, came John Locke, whose political and religious views had put him out of sympathy with his Oxford colleagues ten years before, and whose intimacy with Shaftesbury had injured his innocent reputation at the time of the Popish Plot and the intrigues with Monmouth. Locke had prudently withdrawn to Holland for the last six years before the accession of William III. He now returned under the protection of a government more congenial to his own way of thinking than any he had known in England.

3 · John Locke, 1632–1704

Locke was not a devotee of the academic life. Although an inveterate writer of letters, and, as a young man, the author of unpublished treatises on political theory, he published nothing until after the Revolution of 1688, when he was fifty-six. Actively interested in all the controversial questions of his age, he was a man of affairs, much involved in politics during a confused and exciting time.

He was born at Wrington, Somerset, near Bristol. His father was a lawyer and small landowner, his mother the daughter of a local tanner. Both parents were of Puritan descent. Although the profession of lawyer was not much respected at that time, the family had an established social position, and Locke's grandfather had been a wealthy clothier.

John was the eldest of three boys, of which the second died in infancy. The third, five years John's junior, died in 1663, by which time both the parents had died. Locke found himself alone in the world at the age of thirty-one. His feeling for his father had been one of great 'respect and affection'; the relation between them seems to have been very much that which, in the *Thoughts Concerning Education*, Locke says is proper between father and son – firmness at first, with less reserve and more intimacy as the son grew older.

From his father he inherited some land and house property, which, together with investments in the slave trade, brought him a modest competence for the rest of his life, so that, for example, he was able through most of his life to maintain a personal valet-cum-secretary. Though he was never affluent, he was never forced to be completely dependent on a patron. This fact is important, because it secured his personal status in his friendships with highly placed people, especially with Lord Shaftesbury.

In the Civil War, Locke's father sided with Parliament, and for a short time served as a captain in the Parliamentary army. This circumstance enabled him to get John into Westminster School in 1647, which the Parliament had taken under its control.

At that time Westminster was ruled by the redoubtable Dr Richard Busby, who was head master for fifty-seven years from 1638 until 1695, when he was nearly ninety. The present Head of Westminster, John Carleton, writes of Busby: '. . . through times of exceptional difficulty and danger, he steered the destinies of the school with whole-hearted devotion and apparently unfailing judgment. When he died in 1695 his name had become a household word, and the terror of his rod proverbial. He had successfully survived the Civil War, the Commonwealth, the Restoration and the Revolution, serving three dynasties and witnessing three changes of worship, and each danger surmounted had left the school stronger than before.'[1] One of his methods of dealing with inconvenient political situations was to report sick when asked to subscribe to unwelcome doctrines, such as the Presbyterian Covenant. His own sympathies remained Royalist; and the school's monarchist flavour certainly broadened Locke's outlook, contrasting as it did with his Puritan background.

Dr Busby was not only a renowned flagellator but a dramatically effective teacher. Richard Steele, though not himself educated at Westminster, wrote: 'He had a power of raising what the lad had in him to the utmost height in what Nature designed him'; and he believed that 'Busby's genius for education has as great an effect upon the age he lived in as that of any ancient Philosopher, without excepting one, had upon his contemporaries.'

On the other hand, there is some evidence that the work of the school suffered a good deal through shortage of teaching staff in the latter years of Busby's reign; this decline, however, would have been long after John Locke left. However that may be, Locke did not enjoy his time at Westminster, and it is clear from the *Thoughts* that he took a poor view of schools in general. There can be little doubt that, by our standards, the best schools of the seventeenth century were bad. They were grim places in which to live. The day began at 5.15 a.m., and there was little respite until bed-time. On the other hand, there was little attempt to regulate or control the boys' behaviour outside the hours of formal instruction. Schools were places of instruction; and the ideals of Thomas Arnold, which have done so much to leaven our notion of the meaning and scope of education, lay far in the future.

In 1652, at the age of twenty, Locke went up to Christ Church, Oxford, with a scholarship. It was exceptional in those days to enter the university so late; many undergraduates went up at fourteen, and the routine was like a continuation of school – the day began at 5.0 a.m., and there was a heavy programme of compulsory lectures.

Locke took his B.A. in 1656 and his M.A. in 1658. He was immediately elected to a Senior Studentship (i.e. a fellowship) at Christ Church; in 1660 he was appointed Lecturer in Greek, and in 1662 Lecturer on Rhetoric. He was a conscientious lecturer and tutor.

When Locke went up to Oxford, the Dean of Christ Church was John Owen, a liberal-minded believer in toleration. Locke himself, although he became strongly liberal in later years, was at this stage royalist and right-wing. In 1660 he wrote: 'A general freedom is but a general bondage.' His political ideas were undoubtedly influenced by Thomas Hobbes, author of the *Leviathan*, though Locke never acknowledged his debt to Hobbes.* His later liberalism was partly the result of his disappointment with the Clarendon Code, which created the machinery for persecuting dissenters after

---

* The case against Locke for having borrowed from Hobbes without acknowledgement is not as strong as has been represented. It is true that, inside the cover of Locke's copy of Velschius: *Sylloge Observationum* (1672), Locke has copied a passage from Hobbes' *Leviathan* with no acknowledgement of the source. But Mr Peter Laslett points out that this is the only instance known to him of any quotation from Hobbes in all Locke's papers, and also that Locke's usual practice was to be scrupulously accurate in noting his references.

the Restoration in 1660, partly the effect of Shaftesbury's influence after 1667, and partly due to the example of toleration in Brandenburg where he spent some time in 1665.

The restoration of the monarchy in 1660 discouraged liberalism at Oxford. Dr John Fell, who became Dean of Christ Church, was a strong royalist. To him is due the credit for toughening the discipline at Christ Church at a time when there was much loose living at Oxford; in some colleges both dons and undergraduates were grossly dissolute.

Locke was repelled by the Aristotelian tradition in philosophy then prevalent in Oxford, and was drawn towards Bacon and Descartes. Descartes was then becoming the leading philosopher in Europe; and Locke's first serious interest in philosophy came from reading his writings (which he began to do about 1666), and even more from the writings of Gassendi, to whom he never acknowledged his obligation. Locke eagerly accepted Descartes' method of systematic doubt. But he went with Gassendi rather than with Descartes in his thoroughgoing insistence on the inductive, empirical approach to knowledge, which is the method of modern science. His *Essay Concerning Human Understanding* was directed at least partly against Descartes.

Locke, however, was not drawn to a life of scholarship. He was always too much interested in the affairs of the world to be a bookworm. As an undergraduate he had no great respect for authority, and was reputed to prefer witty company to serious study.

As a college don he resisted the normal requirement of those days to take Holy Orders. Not that he lacked religious belief; he published important works on Christianity in 1695 and 1697. His religion was latitudinarian or rationalistic, in sympathy with the school of Cambridge Platonists who, in Bishop Burnet's words, 'declared against superstition on the one hand and enthusiasm on the other'. He came to believe in toleration for all but those whose beliefs would by their nature destroy freedom. These included atheists (because they had no proper basis for morality), and members of religions who claimed allegiance to a foreign power (including Roman Catholics). His motives for his belief in freedom were at least as much political as spiritual; he had seen toleration operating in the Netherlands, and knew the divisive and destructive effect of religious persecution. When his opinions had settled down, he had for the rest of his life a healthy distrust of two mental states: on the one hand, an unthinking addiction to tradition (characteristic of royalism); on the other hand, excessive emotional zeal (characteristic of Puritanism).

Locke wanted a broad, comprehensive Church, with a minimal theology. Christianity was, for him, a reasonable faith, unnecessarily complicated by the theologians. While revelation might go beyond reason, nothing in Christian revelation contradicted reason. Locke believed that reason could prove God's existence, but that more than reason was needed to apprehend God's nature. There was a genuine intuitive piety in Locke's nature. His attitude towards Scripture (shown especially in his study of St Paul's Epistles) entitles him to be regarded as a forerunner of the modern critical approach to Biblical study.

In 1660 Locke was prepared to welcome the restoration of the Established Church; in this attitude he was no doubt influenced by the fact that most of his friends had royalist sympathies. He was soon deeply disappointed, however, by the policy of enforced conformity enshrined in the Clarendon Code. Between the Restoration of 1660 and the Revolution of 1688, the nation was lacerated by the systematic persecution of the large body of Protestant nonconformists. John Bunyan and George Fox were among those who suffered ruin and imprisonment rather than conform. Merchants were alarmed, and trade discouraged, by the penalties imposed on dissenters. Education was hampered by the exclusion of dissenting schoolmasters from corporate towns.

Locke was so versatile that it is difficult to say where his main concerns lay. It would seem, however, that his chief interests were in science and medicine. It has been suggested that he studied medicine in order to retain his Christ Church Studentship without taking Holy Orders. To some extent this may have been a motive. But there is no reason to doubt Locke's sincere interest in science and medicine. His *Herbarium* (the study of plants was closely related to that of medicine) is a wonderful labour of love, consisting of some 3,000 plants, dated and annotated, and pressed between sheets of his pupils' written exercises. These flowers, beautifully preserved, may be among the earliest surviving specimens of English wild flowers. Locke was, moreover, well acquainted with the founders of the Royal Society, including Robert Boyle in particular. His friendship with Thomas Sydenham reinforced his special interest in medicine. He was himself elected a Fellow of the Royal Society in 1668. By that time the Society had 200 members; but many were aristocratic and wealthy amateurs.

Soon after 1660, when Locke inherited his father's property, lost his only surviving brother, and was thus left alone in the world, there was an interlude when he left the university and entered public service. As secretary to Sir Walter Vane, he accompanied him on a diplomatic mission to the Elector of Brandenburg in 1665. The object of the exercise was to secure the Elector's help, or at least his neutrality, in the war against the Dutch. The mission failed because the Elector wanted more money than the British Government would pay; and Locke returned to England in the following year. In Brandenburg Locke found that Calvinists, Lutherans, and Roman Catholics were all tolerated. In his own words: 'They quietly permit one another to choose their way to heaven.' This experience must have influenced Locke's thinking powerfully towards toleration.

At that time, and some time later, Locke had some thoughts of marriage. By no means indifferent to feminine charm, he had some youthful flirtations and wrote some ardent letters. Nor were his flirtations confined to his earlier years. But he remained a bachelor all his life, and does not seem to have regretted it.

On his return to Oxford in 1666 he renewed his friendship with Boyle and the others who were active in the Royal Society, and devoted himself to medical and scientific studies. He applied in 1666 for the degree of Doctor of Medicine, but was deservedly unsuccessful because he tried to by-pass the course for the degree of Bachelor of Medicine by using influence with Lord Clarendon, Chancellor of the University. In this attempt Shaftesbury may have

C

helped him. The Faculty of Medicine, however, turned down the application. At the same time his Studentship at Christ Church was made permanent by royal warrant, and he received a dispensation releasing him from the obligation to take Holy Orders. In 1667 he met and worked with Thomas Sydenham, whose experimental approach to medicine was very congenial to Locke. A second try for the M.D. failed in 1670; but in 1674 Locke was made Bachelor of Medicine with licence to practise as a physician. He was now secure in his position, both as a don at Christ Church and as a practising physician.

A fateful chapter in Locke's career began when, in 1666, he first met Lord Shaftesbury, then Anthony Ashley Cooper, at Oxford. An unlikely, but firm and lasting, friendship was formed between Locke and this extraordinary political buccaneer, whom G. M. Trevelyan described as 'the man destined first to found the Whig Party and then to ruin it by furious driving'.

In 1667 Locke accepted Ashley's invitation to be his personal physician, and to live at Exeter House, Strand, Ashley's London home. Ashley had for twelve years suffered from an internal abscess. After consultation with Sydenham and others, Locke got a surgeon-barber to open Ashley's abdomen, and drained the abscess with a tube which Ashley wore for the rest of his life. In spite of the inconvenience involved, Ashley made a remarkable recovery, and probably owed his life to Locke.

Locke also medically attended members of Ashley's family and friends of the family. In spite of the enlightened work of Sydenham and others, medical science was still primitive by our standards. It is surprising to learn that, when he was in France in 1675, Locke gave himself a clyster (enema) because a wooden pole had fallen on his head.

To Ashley, Locke owed to a considerable extent his conversion to a liberal belief in toleration, the encouragement of his scientific interests, and his introduction to a wider world of experience and public affairs.

Locke undertook the conduct of some of Ashley's business for him, as a personal secretary and adviser. Le Clerc tells a story of

Locke as a member of Ashley's household. Three or four distinguished guests were playing cards. Locke took out his pocket-book
and wrote as he watched the players. One of them asked him what
he was writing. Locke replied: 'I am endeavouring to profit, as far
as I am able, in your company ... and I thought I could not do
better than write down your conversation. I have written down
what has been said for this past hour or two.' The card table was
abandoned.

Locke was also entrusted with the education of Ashley's son, then
a boy of fifteen or sixteen. The boy was a disappointment to his
father, being neither intelligent nor physically healthy. Locke was
later employed to negotiate his marriage. Some years afterwards,
the grandson, born of this marriage, was placed in Locke's care
from the age of three until he was sent to Winchester at the age of
twelve. The boy was taught by a governess under Locke's general
direction.

In 1672 Ashley was created Earl of Shaftesbury and appointed
Lord Chancellor. In the same year Shaftesbury gave Locke the
minor public office of Secretary of Presentations of Benefices,
which carried a salary of £500 a year and involved attending to
Church business under the Chancellor's control.

In the same year Locke was given a post in the reconstructed
Council of Trade and Plantations under Shaftesbury's presidency
and became its secretary in the next year. The hazards of his asso-
ciation with Shaftesbury, however, already made themselves felt;
for in that year, 1673, Shaftesbury was dismissed from his office of
Lord Chancellor. By 1674 Locke had lost both his government posts
and had no prospect of further official employment. But Shaftesbury
gave him an annuity of £100.

Locke had visited France in 1672. By 1675 his health was not
good, and he got leave of absence from Christ Church and went to
Montpellier, at that time a resort of invalids. He was suffering from
asthma as early as 1670. The fact that he believed this complaint to
be pulmonary tuberculosis must have put an added strain upon him.

Except for local visits, he stayed at Montpellier until 1677. In that
year he went to Paris, to take charge (at the request of Shaftesbury

who was now imprisoned in the Tower) of a son of Sir John Banks, one of Shaftesbury's city friends. This tutorship lasted two years, but little is known of it. One year was spent in Paris, and in the summer of 1678 Locke took the boy on a journey to Rome, but turned back owing to the condition of the Alpine passes. They accordingly returned to Paris until April 1679, when Locke came back to England, where Shaftesbury, released from the Tower and appointed President of the Privy Council, again wanted Locke's services.

It is characteristic of Locke's many-sidedness that, during his time in France, he wrote to Shaftesbury on gardening, offering to send plants, and giving an account of vine and olive growing – a study which was published many years later. He corresponded with Boyle about scientific instruments; and also studied political institutions and antiquities. At Montpellier he met Thomas Herbert, afterwards Earl of Pembroke. To him Locke dedicated the *Essay Concerning Human Understanding*, written at this time but published later.

By 1679 Shaftesbury's fortunes were changed rapidly. In October of that year he was dismissed from office, and became involved in political intrigues until his flight to Holland at the end of 1682. During this time Locke was in close touch with Shaftesbury, and in 1679–80 spent some time at Thanet House, now Shaftesbury's London residence. During 1680–1 Locke was superintending the education of Shaftesbury's grandson, afterwards the third Earl, and was engaged in various business of Shaftesbury's. An ardent supporter of the Protestant cause, Shaftesbury, as we have seen, was involved in revolutionary plots which led to his re-arrest in 1681 and his flight early in 1683 to Holland, where he died soon after.

Although Locke sympathized with Shaftesbury's opposition to Popery and arbitrary government, there is no clear evidence that he was concerned in any of the plots. It is a plausible theory that his visit to France in 1675 was partly to assist Shaftesbury's intrigues with the French Government against Danby; the Whigs agreed to moderate their opposition to France and the Duke of York in return for money. After his return to England, Locke was certainly in close correspondence with Shaftesbury, gave him information on political matters and went on errands for him, up to the time of Shaftesbury's flight to Holland. Beyond that, there is no proof of Locke's involvement. At the same time, he was far too cautious to have left any recorded evidence. His own departure from England in the autumn of 1683 was certainly hurried, and preceded by the destruction of a quantity of papers.

Whatever view one takes, it is clear that his close connexion with Shaftesbury was bound to bring Locke under a good deal of suspicion. Oxford looked at him askance; the University condemned the doctrine that resistance to the king could be lawful. Christ Church was no place for a man suspected of intriguing against Church and King. Some anonymous pamphlets were attributed to him, and it was generally believed that he was implicated in the Rye House Plot.

Locke's position in England became so uncomfortable that, in the autumn of 1683, he followed Shaftesbury to Holland, and spent the next six years in voluntary exile. He liked the cleanliness of Holland as compared with France, and found the life there both socially and politically congenial. There was religious toleration, and Locke found himself in tune with the sect of the Remonstrants, who believed in a rational theology and minimal creeds.

In spite of the anxieties and preoccupations of the years 1679–83 in England, Locke had practised to a limited extent as a physician, transcribed some of Sydenham's notes, and written his *Treatise on Government*. In the autumn of 1684, when he was in Holland, Locke was deprived of his Christ Church Studentship, though the Dean, Dr Fell, reported quite fairly that there was no evidence against him. The form of the dismissal was a summons to return to his post in the college, and, on Locke's refusal, his expulsion.

Locke moved about in Holland, to avoid appearing to associate with those concerned in plotting Monmouth's Rebellion. Whatever the truth may have been, Locke was believed to be in complicity with English plotters against the English monarchy, and attempts were made to get the Netherlands Government to extradite him. At one time he judged it prudent to go into hiding under an assumed name. Later, on representations by William Penn and Lord Pembroke, James II offered to receive and pardon him for complicity in Monmouth's plot. Characteristically, Locke declined to be pardoned for a crime which he had not committed.

For some time he lived at Rotterdam, and became known to William and Mary of Orange, who thought highly of him. He was also received into a distinguished literary circle in Holland, and did much writing, including (in Latin) *A Letter Concerning Toleration* (translated and published in 1690), and the letters to Edward Clarke which were later published as *Some Thoughts Concerning Education*.

The Revolution of 1688 was Locke's signal to return to England. He made the journey in the company of William and Mary, landing at Greenwich on 12 February 1688, in a ship whose flag bore the motto: *Pro Religione et Libertate*. As soon as he was proclaimed king, William III offered Locke the post of ambassador to the Elector of Brandenburg; but Locke refused on grounds of ill-health, and because he did not feel equal to the hard drinking that accompanied German diplomacy. He was given the modest office of Commissioner of Appeals (almost a sinecure) at £200 a year. He withdrew a petition for the restoration of his Christ Church Studentship because he realized that it would disturb the college and displace his successor.

It was in 1689 that Locke first met that strange, untidy genius, Isaac Newton. For a time Locke lived in London. But he found the smoke intolerable to his asthma, and in 1691 he moved to High Laver, Essex, to the house of Sir Francis Masham, whose second wife was a Cudworth. Edward Clarke, to whom the letters on education were written, was a common friend of Locke and the Cudworths. The Mashams had an infant son, and consulted Locke on his upbringing. Locke probably found Lady Masham a much more interesting and intelligent friend than her good-natured but rather boring husband, Sir Francis.

In 1696 a new Council of Trade was established, and Locke was appointed a member with a salary of £1,000 a year. It met five times a week, and in spite of failing health Locke attended frequently during the summer and autumn. He prepared a number of schemes, including a plan for promoting the Irish linen industry and for reforming the Poor Laws (both were abortive). The work of the Council of Trade attracted Locke as much for its intrinsic importance as it did by reason of the handsome salary. But his health was not up to the strain; he tried to resign in the winter of 1697, but hung on until 1700. During those years, not only was he a full-time civil servant but he was also engaged in political and theological controversy, and was the victim of some libellous attacks in the course of the pamphleteering that was going on. His publications, and his involvement in controversy, brought Locke for the first time the full recognition as an author that he deserved. He did not find fame always agreeable.

From 1700 onwards Locke was afflicted by other ailments besides asthma. These included a painful swelling of the legs, and from 1700 till 1703 deafness. Nevertheless, he was interested in people and affairs to the last, and there was no decline of his mental powers. He died on 28 October 1704 at High Laver, and was buried there. As he lay dying he received the sacrament, and at his request had psalms read to him. He left estate worth about £20,000, and bequeathed to the Bodleian Library, Oxford, all his published works, including those published anonymously.

Locke's most important works were published between 1690 and 1695. One obvious reason for the long delay in publication of works, many of which were planned and drafted years before, was that Locke's views were less publicly acceptable before 1689 than after the Revolution, especially his political views.

An Essay Concerning Human Understanding. First published 1690, though drafted twenty years before as an outcome of informal discussions between half a dozen friends. Further editions followed in 1694, 1695, 1699, and 1706. The book caused a considerable stir, and few books on philosophy have made headway so fast. In 1692 the *Essay* was recommended for students of Trinity College, Dublin. The official reception in Oxford was different. In 1703 the Heads of Oxford Colleges agreed that tutors should *not* read the book with their students. But the prohibition proved to be a most effective advertisement. The *Conduct of the Understanding*, published after Locke's death, was an extension of the *Essay*, with special attention to the problems of clear thinking.

Two Treatises on Government, and *Letters on Toleration*. Published 1690, but not written after 1688, as often supposed, to justify the Revolution. Locke's theories in these essays supplied the Whigs with their political philosophy for the next generation. In the *Treatises on Government* Locke presented his version of the Social Contract theory, in which 'preservation of property' was the 'chief end' of political society, the functions of the State were minimal, and the basic principle of government was consent. In connexion with Toleration, it must be remembered that this was a very live, practical issue at that time; the nature and degree of civil and religious freedom, and of governmental authority, were no mere academic problems.

Some Considerations of the Lowering of Interest and Raising the Value of Money. Published 1692 (mostly written in 1668). Locke's most important book on economics.

Some Thoughts Concerning Education. Published 1693. The substance of this work was in letters written from Holland to Edward Clarke in 1684.

The Reasonableness of Christianity. Published anonymously in 1695. Locke was vehemently attacked for his views in this book, and he replied to his critics in two *Vindications* (1695, 1697). In these writings he struck the keynote of the most popular theology of the eighteenth century as represented by the broad-church clergy. Locke's theological position at times appeared virtually unitarian; but he remained a member of the Anglican Church.

These are only a few of Locke's writings. A complete list would number some twenty publications, some consisting of several items. The first collected edition of his works appeared in 1714, ten years after his death.

The few works here mentioned, however, are enough to illustrate Locke's effective influence in philosophy, theology and politics. Locke's authority as a philosopher was unrivalled in England for half a century and more after his death. John Stuart Mill (1806–

73), who is properly regarded as Locke's spiritual descendant, described him as 'the unquestioned founder of the analytic philosophy of mind'.[2] There is no doubt that Locke's work, with its emphasis on the empirical approach, contributed powerfully to the emergence of a scientific psychology, although in Locke's own time psychology as a science had not been clearly differentiated from philosophy.

There are enough extant portraits of Locke to give us a reliable impression of his appearance. He had a long face, rather like that of a well-bred horse – the nose long and bony, with delicate, open nostrils, the upper lip longish, the mouth with a hint of a smile at the corners, the chin round and firm, and the cheek bones high and prominent. The grey eyes, under rather heavy lids, are well spaced, and the brows wide and strongly marked. In contrast with the mouth, the eyes do not smile, but look at life steadily and rather sceptically. Three of the portraits, by different painters, closely resemble one another; and the inference therefore is that they are like the sitter. These are the paintings by John Greenhill (probably done in 1672 when Locke was forty), by Herman Verelst (done in 1689), and by Michael Dahl (done about 1696). The Greenhill and the Verelst are believed to have been given to Edward Clarke. There is a miniature, drawn (perhaps in 1685) by Sylvester Brownower, who acted as servant and secretary to Locke for some years; it is an attractive drawing, but less recognizably like the other portraits, although there is evidence that the Mashams thought it a good likeness. Kneller painted Locke twice. The earlier portrait (1697) is lost, though there are many copies; the later one (1704) shows Locke pathetically old and ill. This last portrait was painted at the Mashams' house at High Laver, and was a gift to Anthony Collins, to whom Locke characteristically wrote: 'Pray get Sir Godfrey to write . . . on the backside of mine, John Locke 1704. This he did on Mr Molyneux's and mine, the last he drew, and this is necessary to be done, as else the pictures of private persons are lost in two or three generations and so the picture loses of its value, it being not known whom it was made to represent.'[3]

The outstanding features of Locke's character were modesty,

common sense, humour, and loyalty to the truth. He believed in virtue with all the strength of his Puritan background. He was a man of temperate habits and careful morals. But he also had warm and ready sympathy, especially towards children (possibly because he had none of his own). He objected strongly to bad manners. He was, moreover, a man of great industry who spared himself nothing in order to complete a task thoroughly. Indefatigable in his indexing and annotating, his scrupulous care in all he undertook justifies Mr Laslett's comment that Locke's 'genius was a genius for the infinite taking of pains'.*

Locke also had some less admirable qualities. He did not always recognize his debt to thinkers who influenced him. And for one of such common sense, he had a curious passion for secrecy. Maurice Cranston, in his fine biography of Locke, writes: 'Locke is an elusive subject for a biographer because he was an extremely secretive man. He modified a system of shorthand for the purposes of concealment; he employed all sorts of curious little cyphers; he cut signatures and other identifiable names from letters he preserved; at one time he used invisible ink.'[4]

Locke seems to have been a fairly typical conscientious introvert, by no means lacking in courage, but making life harder for himself than it need have been by a somewhat distrustful outlook. This view is confirmed by his portraits, with their contrast between the humorous mouth and the almost apprehensive eyes. Some would say that it is also confirmed by his asthma and by the fact that, in his own words, he was 'naturally costive'.

Locke's writings reveal a belief in toleration and a devotion to the cause of civil liberty. His style, like the man himself, rejected anything obscure or speculative.

Locke is an attractively lucid writer, sometimes eloquent, often amusing. He is by no means always consistent; indeed, consistency could hardly be expected of one who wrote so much and at the same time lived so actively. It is often pointed out that Locke did not always see the full implications of his own ideas; had he done so, he might not have been so effective a prophet and pioneer.

* *The Times Literary Supplement*, 11 March 1960.

For students of education there is significance in the very fact that Locke was a man of many interests, who explored many fields of knowledge. Standing on the threshold of the modern world of scientific inquiry, he still belonged to an age before the fragmentation of human knowledge into many self-contained and mutually unintelligible departments. Locke was a 'full man' in an age when it was still possible for a man of good intellect to grasp the wholeness of human thought and knowledge. The universities of his day knew nothing of Lord Snow's 'Two Cultures'. It is interesting to speculate on what Locke would have thought of our own disintegration of the academic map, when it is not only a case of a biologist being out of communication with, say, a medieval historian, but rather of experts in one branch of biology being out of touch with experts in other branches of biology. In this age no one can aspire to know every 'subject'. But we can at least try to understand the sort of questions which the different branches of knowledge ask and seek to answer. In this way we may work towards the achievement of a whole view of life. Without such understanding, there can be no true education.

NOTES ON TWO OF LOCKE'S FRIENDS

I. ROBERT BOYLE, 1627–92

The Hon. Robert Boyle was the seventh son of the Earl of Cork. As a boy at Eton he was made ill by an apothecary's administration of a wrong dose, an experience which made him 'fear physicians more than the disease'. Being of an active and curious turn of mind, he was not content to shun the medical profession, but sought to penetrate the mysteries in which they were so often at fault. Hence his interest in medical matters and in science generally. He was one of the earliest members of the Royal Society.

In an age when chemical knowledge was in a very muddled state, and most of the views held had no proven basis in fact, Boyle was a very careful experimenter. John Locke recognized a kindred spirit in Boyle with his disciplined empirical approach to knowledge.

In 1661 Boyle published the *Sceptical Chemist*, a title which designated one who questions everything and takes nothing for granted. The book was in the form of a dialogue between the Sceptical Chemist and two other characters – one a disciple of Aristotle who thought in terms of the four elements, earth, air, fire, and water; the other a disciple of Paracelsus (*c.* A.D. 1500) who believed in three 'principles', sulphur, mercury, and salt. The book described many of Boyle's experiments; and the main theme was the attempt to discover, by experiment, what substances are *elements* (i.e. substances that cannot be further split up).

Boyle did not, in fact, discover much that was new. But like Sydenham, his approach was revolutionary. It was not until a hundred years later that the theory of chemical elements finally displaced the phlogiston theory. (Phlogiston was the 'fire' element under another name; everything that would burn contained phlogiston.) But when the advance eventually came, it was on lines projected by Boyle. He may be considered to have foreshadowed the work of Dalton and the Swedish chemist Berzelius, who worked out atomic weights of elements and a system of classification.

Both Boyle and Newton were ahead of Lavoisier (a century later) in their view of heat. Lavoisier included heat and light as 'elements', and thought they were invisible and weightless fluids. Boyle and Newton regarded heat as due to motion of some sort.

Robert Boyle's delicate, thoughtful face can be seen, in a copy after Johann Kerseboom, at the National Portrait Gallery.

2. THOMAS SYDENHAM, 1624–89

At this time England was seething with conflict between superstition and science, between the tyranny of preconceived ideas and the evidence of experiment. In medicine particularly, the seventeenth century was an age of quacks, mountebanks, nostrums and patent medicines, alchemy and witchcraft. Extraordinary and repulsive ingredients (such as human sweat, animal excreta) were used in medicines.

Meanwhile, at an academic level, a good deal of anatomical study, by microscope and by dissection, was going on, but was making very little impact on medical practice.

Sydenham had two main and closely related objectives. One was to use empirical methods to dispel superstition and make medicine scientific. 'In writing, therefore, a history of diseases, every philosophical hypothesis which hath prejudiced the writer in its favour ought to be totally laid aside, and then the manifest and natural phenomena of diseases, however minute, must be noted with the utmost accuracy . . . For 'tis difficult to give a detail of the errors that spring from hypotheses, whilst writers, misled by these, assign such phenomena for diseases as never existed but in their own brains.' Sydenham's other aim was to bring the best available knowledge into actual medical practice – i.e. to the bedside.

Although he made no historic discovery, Sydenham was the first to embark on the systematic analysis and classification of actual cases of disease. He has left vivid first-hand accounts of the clinical course of diseases (e.g. gout), which have remained models of the clinical method to the present day. He may be said to have founded modern clinical medicine.

A bluff, vigorous man, Sydenham looks very much alive in Mary Beale's portrait (1688). He published a number of books both in Latin and in English, of which the most notable is *Methodus Curandi Febres* (1665), dedicated to Robert Boyle. He was not in London at the time of the Great Plague of 1665. But he studied many other fevers, including scarlatina, measles, bronchopneumonia, dysentery, as well as malaria, which was common in England at that time. He popularized the use of quinine in those fevers which respond to it.

A great admirer of Hippocrates, he believed in the curative power of Nature, as the opening sentence of his book on fevers shows: 'A disease, in my opinion, how prejudicial soever its courses may be to the body, is no more than a vigorous effort of Nature to throw off the morbific matter, and thus recover the patient.'

In medicine, Sydenham stands for three things:

a] The empirical approach

When Sir Hans Sloane as a young man came to Sydenham with a glowing letter of introduction, extolling him as a botanist and anatomist, Sydenham brushed it aside with: 'This is all very fine, but it won't do! Anatomy! Botany! Nonsense! Sir, I know an old woman in Covent Garden who understands botany better. And, as for anatomy, my butcher can dissect a joint full as well. No, young man, all this is stuff: you must go to the bedside; it is there alone you can learn disease.'

b] Belief in the curative power of Nature

His admiration of Hippocrates has been noted. He insisted on fresh air in the sick room – a prescription which some modern hospitals might observe with advantage. He recommended horse riding. And he advised strongly against over-dosing the patient; if you don't know what to do, do nothing.

c] He anticipated the germ theory of disease

Although Sydenham did not himself reach the germ theory, his idea of infectious conditions as specific entities prepared the way for it.

One should not be surprised at the slow rate of scientific progress in those days. Not only had the principles and methods of scientific inquiry to battle their way against prejudice and superstition, but (perhaps even more important) the means of disseminating knowledge were primitive by our standards. In these days when news goes round the world almost instantaneously by radio and television, it is difficult to re-create in imagination the very different conditions when books were comparatively few, and travel and communication were immensely more difficult. It was a world in which, by our standards, news crawled.

PART TWO

Locke's Philosophy

The three chapters that follow are an attempt to set forth the main features of Locke's thought. First, there is a brief description of his general philosophy, as presented in the Essay Concerning Human Understanding *and the* Conduct of the Understanding. *Then comes a summary of his ideas about education, followed by a sketch of the background of English educational thought and practice against which Locke's work has to be seen.*

4 · Reason and Experience –
Locke's Theory of Knowledge

The chief purpose of this book is to discuss Locke's ideas about education. It has already been made clear that education was only one of his many interests. His views on politics and religion emerge, I hope, incidentally – mainly in the outline of his life. But his philosophical writings deserve more than incidental reference, partly because it is in this field that his greatest historical importance lies, and partly because an understanding of his views on education requires some knowledge of his philosophical position.

The aim of this chapter, however, is very limited. Philosophy is a difficult and highly technical field of study. A full discussion of Locke's philosophical writings would involve problems which the ordinary reader is hardly equipped to cope with – for example, the many senses in which the term 'idea' can be used, and the relation between language and meaning. All that I am attempting in this chapter is to give the general reader an indication of the main problem with which Locke is concerned in the *Essay*, and of Locke's place in the history of philosophical thought.

Those who want to study further Locke's philosophy can profitably read Richard I. Aaron's *John Locke* (O.U.P., 2nd edn, 1955), or D. J. O'Connor's *John Locke* (Penguin Books, 1952).

It has been said that, in the history of human thought, the right questions are more important than the answers. Professor A. J. Ayer says of Locke: 'His genius as a philosopher was above all a gift for raising the important questions.'[1] Summing up Locke's contribution to philosophy, Professor Aaron says: 'His writings secured for posterity the advances which had been made by the most radical and progressive elements of society in the seventeenth century. He consolidated the advanced positions . . . Locke's works dominated the English mind in the first half of the eighteenth century, and his influence was almost as great in America and in France.'[2] It should be remembered, however, that Locke was never a doctrinaire radical. He was too English, and had too much practical common sense. For him politics were the art of the possible; lover of liberty as he was, he rejected republicanism and total toleration. In his purely philosophical thinking there was always a tension between the continuing influence of the intellectual tradition in which he was brought up and the new insights which belonged to the age of modern science. In speaking of 'philosophy' and 'science' as distinct disciplines, we must remember that in Locke's day there was no such distinction. Locke would have regarded his friends Newton, Sydenham, and Boyle as philosophers equally with Descartes. It is largely for this reason that psychology, as a science, took so long to separate itself from metaphysics and logic.

The *Essay Concerning Human Understanding*, of which three preliminary drafts are extant, grew gradually, and was worked over for many years. It therefore has not the clarity and consistency that might be expected of a single piece of writing completed at one time.

Locke belonged to the new rational, scientific age in his strong belief in Reason and the empirical approach to knowledge. The purpose of the *Essay Concerning Human Understanding* is 'to inquire into the original, certainty, and extent of human knowledge, together with the grounds and degrees of belief, opinion and assent'. By 'knowledge', Locke meant what Professor Gilbert Ryle has distinguished as 'knowing that' as contrasted with 'knowing how'. By the 'original', Locke meant the sources of knowledge; his discussion of this question led to his rejection of the traditional view that a mysterious innate knowledge existed. In his examination of 'certainty' he considered the contemporary assumption that all knowledge had to conform to the pattern of the syllogism, and also the misleading effects of vague and pretentious language. The exploration of the 'extent' of knowledge was aimed at excluding problems which, because they are beyond our power to solve, it is expedient to leave alone.

In brief his answer to the problem is that knowledge comes to us through experience, ordered by reason. 'In that (i.e. in experience) all our knowledge is founded, and from that it ultimately derives itself.' John Stuart Mill described Locke as 'the unquestioned founder of the analytic philosophy of mind'. His emphasis on experience paved the way for a scientific psychology in place of metaphysical speculation.

The attempt to reconcile thoroughgoing empiricism with thoroughgoing faith in reason is not without its difficulties. On the one hand, having denied the 'innate ideas' of traditional philosophy and (in some contexts) affirmed that the mind is a blank apart from the impressions that are made on it from without, Locke has to moderate this extreme empiricism by recognizing innate 'powers' for discriminating, comparing, and generalizing sense impressions. Reason, in fact, is 'the candle of the Lord set up by Himself in men's minds'. Natural reason is the touchstone 'to distinguish substantial gold from superficial glitterings, truth from appearances'. On the other hand, he has to recognize the frailty of reason, and his analysis of the sources of error is penetrating. Although he relies heavily on reason in the formation of character (the will 'never fails in its obedience to the dictates of the understanding'), he recognizes that some men never reason at all, but follow the example of others; some 'put passion in the place of reason' (these 'commonly content themselves with words which have no distinct ideas to them'); some sincerely try to reason, but never attain a full view of all that relates to the question. No man is free from limitation of view: 'therefore it is no wonder we conclude not right from our partial views'.

From these difficulties Locke is, as on most occasions, saved by his common sense, which prevails over the subtleties of argument. In particular, he insists that natural reason must be *exercised*. Want of exercise 'weakens and extinguishes this noble faculty in us'; and he gives two telling examples: 'a country gentleman who, leaving

Latin and learning in the university, removes thence to his mansion-house and associates with neighbours of the same strain, who relish nothing but hunting and a bottle'; or 'one muffled up in the zeal and infallibility of his own sect and will not touch a book or enter into debate with a person that will question any of those things which to him are sacred'.

In his belief in reason and the empirical method, Locke belongs to the age of modern science. Characteristic of the age is belief in *natural law*, formulated by reason on a basis of empirical observation. With the work of Copernicus, Kepler, and Newton, who discovered and demonstrated the operation of natural law, Locke was wholly in sympathy. He may be said to have founded a tradition of inquiry into the nature of truth which, broadly speaking, has persisted in this country to the present time.

The essence of Locke's thought is his theory of knowledge. To understand his contribution, it is necessary to look at the traditional philosophy against which he rebelled.

Plato asked how ideas entered the mind. In terms of virtue, he asked whether virtue was a gift of the gods or a type of conduct acquired through education. Here, in fact, is the origin of the age-old dialectic of nature and nurture. Plato decided for *innate ideas* on the grounds that, if one had no previous knowledge of virtue, how could one find or recognize it? Plato, however, allowed something for *experience*. The ideas, though innate, are not fully developed but are indistinct replicas of the perfect ideas existing in the eternal realm. When a child is born, these ideas are obscured. From then on, learning is a process of reminiscence. Sense-experience serves to arouse corresponding ideas that have lain dormant since birth. Always suspicious of the bodily senses, because of their manifest unreliability, Plato exalted the mind's contribution to knowledge at the expense of that of the senses, regarding the body as a necessary evil in this world.

Aristotle continued Plato's work. The *psyche* was the principle that caused the organism to bring to fulfilment the characteristics latent within it. This principle of growth functioned in five ways ('faculties'): (i) vegetative (simple growth and maintenance), (ii) appetitive (including the desire towards what is true and good), (iii) sensory, (iv) locomotive, (v) rational. For Aristotle, the power to reason was not self-initiating but needed sensory stimulus.

For centuries, controversy was not about the principle of these 'faculties' but about their number. Gradually, Aristotle's five faculties were reduced to the three of knowing, feeling, and willing (the cognitive, affective, and conative functions which are generally accepted in our day). There were also recognized 'faculties' of judgement, memory, imagination, and attention.

These faculties came to be thought of as organs or entities (phrenologists locating them in different parts of the brain). Hence the traditional *faculty psychology*, regarding the faculties as capable of being trained independently of one another. The doctrine of transfer of training was a natural accompaniment.

It is important to distinguish the recognition of various mental functions, such as cognitive, affective, and conative behaviour, from the re-ifying* of mental functions into quasi-organs. It is the latter view which characterizes the faculty psychology which prevailed even into the early part of the present century. Obviously we can say that there is such a thing as 'memory', if all we mean is that we remember. But it is very questionable whether there is such a thing as 'the memory' which can be trained by exercises, as one can develop one's biceps. The tendency to re-ify mental functions has been a source of much error and confusion. Had Locke's lead been better followed, faculty psychology might have been laid to rest a good deal earlier.

The type of thinking associated with faculty psychology also gave the intellect heavy priority over the senses, knowledge derived from sense impression being regarded as very unreliable. *A priori* reasoning was at a premium; the most reliable knowledge was that which could be shown to be *necessarily* so.

---

* To re-ify is to convert mentally into a thing. E.g. the phrase: 'I have a feeling that . . .' simply means: 'I feel that. . . .' If one imagined that this 'feeling' could be somehow located or separately identified, like my hand or my foot, one would be re-ifying it.

Against the Platonic–Aristotelian tradition (prevalent in Locke's day, especially at Oxford, where he encountered it), Locke rebelled. Asking the same question – What is the source of true knowledge? – Locke attacked the doctrine of 'innate ideas'. The source of the mind's 'vast store' is *experience* (basically sense impression). All knowledge derives from observation of the facts of sense experience. The mind is a *tabula rasa*, on which impressions are made. Sweeping away Plato's notion of innate ideas, he maintained that the notions of God, right and wrong, logical propositions like the principle of contradiction, and mathematical axioms, are learnt through the senses – on the grounds that these things are not equally self-evident to all people in all circumstances, and therefore must be the fruits of experience. He went as far as to question the doctrine of Original Sin, holding that children were good or evil according to their education.

It is a natural question, and one often asked, who of Locke's contemporaries were supporting the doctrine of innate ideas in such a way as to provoke such a vigorous attack from Locke. The answer is not very clear, especially as Locke names only one opponent, Lord Herbert of Cherbury. It would seem that Locke had in mind Descartes and his followers (though Descartes did not hold the doctrine as crudely as Locke's attack would imply), to some extent the Cambridge Platonists, and in a general way the traditional teaching at Oxford. In any case, unless the climate of thought had been ripe for Locke's revolt against tradition, his writing would not have caused the stir and exerted the great influence that it did. The reception accorded to Locke's work is the best proof that it was needed.

Locke's attack on the doctrine of innate ideas is a brilliant piece of debating, marked by logical subtlety and felicity of analogy. He considers two types of innate idea: 'speculative maxims' such as the proposition that 'it is impossible for the same thing to be and not to be', and 'practical principles' such as Justice, or 'one should do as he would be done unto'. He is careful to distinguish between the notion of an innate idea, ready-made, so to speak, in the mind, and a law of nature, which may be inherent in the structure of the universe and of which we may by observation and thought attain to knowledge.

The following passages from the *Essay* summarize his conclusions:

'The senses at first let in particular ideas, and furnish this yet empty cabinet, and the mind by degrees growing familiar with some of them, they are lodged in the memory, and names got to them. Afterwards the mind, proceeding further, abstracts them, and by degrees learns the use of general names. In this manner the mind comes to be furnished with ideas and language, the materials about which to exercise its discursive faculty. And the use of reason becomes daily more visible, as these materials that give it employment increase.' (*I ii 15*)

'Our observation, employed either about external sensible objects, or about the internal operations of our minds perceived and reflected on by ourselves, is that which supplies our understandings with all the materials of thinking.' (*II i 2*)

'External objects furnish the mind with the ideas of sensible qualities, which are all those different perceptions they produce in us; and the mind furnishes the understanding with ideas of its own operations.' (*II i 5*)

'And hence we see the reason why it is pretty late before most children get ideas of the operation of their own minds.' (*II i 8*)

Thus Locke reversed the priority of nature over nurture, putting nurture first – environment rather than heredity. But, as is already clear, Locke was not wholly empirical any more than Plato had been wholly the reverse. Plato acknowledged the role of experience in reawakening the innate ideas. And Locke acknowledged the existence of innate 'powers' to organize experience. Thus he maintains that the existence of God and the principles of morality are rationally demonstrable. A good deal of Descartes' systematic rationalism, in fact, remained in Locke's thinking, making his empiricism far from complete. Locke was never a 'sensationist'; he made it quite clear that, in his opinion, sense-experience of itself could not provide us with the full truth even about material things.

The main differences between Locke's view and the traditional view were: (i) his acceptance of sense-experience as a valid and necessary window to reality, as compared with the traditional distrust of the physical senses; (ii) his disregard of 'faculties' as separate entities (in this he was much ahead of his time, since faculty psychology, rejected by Locke and Herbart, continued to be popular into the twentieth century, with its concomitant doctrines of formal training and transfer of training); (iii) his practical enthusiasm for education, which helped to set a new fashion epitomized in Helvetius' 'L'Education peut tout'.

It is interesting to notice the ironical somersault of Locke's down-to-earth empiricism into complete scepticism at the hands of David Hume (1711–76), who pushed Locke's empiricism to the length of refusing to accept any knowledge as valid for which no previous sense impression could be found.★ Thus the notion of cause-and-effect was reduced to temporal sequence, since *post hoc* could be observed, but *propter hoc* could not. Hence scepticism

---

★ In our own day this view has been revived by the logical positivists, who arose in Vienna between the Wars, and are represented in this country by Professor A. J. Ayer. They took the view that questions and answers about the nature of existence and moral obligation (the traditional concerns of metaphysics and moral philosophy) were meaningless because unverifiable. Verifiable statements were of two kinds, either *analytical* (i.e. logically necessary propositions, or tautologies, such as $2 \times 2 = 4$, depending entirely on definitions of the symbols they contain and independent of external references) or *empirical* (established by sense-impression – observation and experiment). 'Metaphysical statements' (about God, free will, etc.,) are neither analytical nor empirical, and therefore are not verifiable.

In recent years, the position of the logical positivists has been considerably modified. Although they still consider that philosophy is mainly concerned with the meaning of language, they no longer say that metaphysical or moral statements are meaningless. Since morality is an indispensable factor in life, these philosophers allow that moral statements have meaning because they have the function of directing conduct. In the modern study of philosophy the importance of the problem of language is fully appreciated. This is, in fact, the subject of Book III of Locke's *Essay*; and, although his analysis would not satisfy a modern philosopher, he deserves full credit for pioneering this field of inquiry.

about the possibility of having any knowledge of reality at all – a result certainly not intended by Locke, though Locke had indeed opened the door by distinguishing between the 'idea' which we perceive and the object represented by that 'idea'. Since the perceived idea is all we can know, we can never know what relation the object itself bears to the idea.

The situation was rescued by Kant (1724–1804), who reinstated *a priori* categories of the mind. Categories of the mind (e.g. causation, time, space) are imposed by the mind upon experience, which can be understood only in terms of these categories. Kant's 'idea(l)-ism' had an interesting and important influence on educational theory, since it emphasized the mind's active agency in manipulating experience, as contrasted with the passive spectator notion of the mind photographing experience, which was one of the less helpful elements in Locke's thought. Rousseau's emphasis on doing rather than knowing is not unrelated to Kant's idea of the mind building from within itself its understanding of the world. It is a pity that Locke, with his clear grasp of the mind's function in organizing experience, did not reach a more dynamic notion of mental activity. The reason may lie in his preoccupation with the theory of knowledge and the cognitive functions generally. At all events, he made too much of the stamping of impressions on the mind, and not enough of the mind's activity in organizing experience.

The following summary is worth quoting from Maurice Cranston's biography of Locke: '*The Essay Concerning Human Understanding* is a very English book, both in its merits and its faults. Its tone is at once moral and pragmatic, its style is homely rather than elegant, its idioms are often commercial. The pursuit of truth, Locke said, "is a duty we owe to God . . . and a duty also we owe our own selves"; utility, for him, was at one with piety. He described Truth as the "proper riches and furniture of the mind", and has indeed been mocked for doing so; but he did not claim to have added to that "stock"; he tried to show the conditions, or some of the conditions, under which the mind could acquire its proper riches and furniture. In this at any rate he abundantly succeeded.'[3]

5 · Locke's Educational Thought

Emphasis on Locke's modernity must not obscure the fact that he stood, at an interesting time in history, between two worlds. His thought has many features of the tradition against which he rebelled.

He gave a new emphasis to the importance of sense-experience. Yet he never fully appreciated the *active* nature of experience and of learning – the importance of the affective and conative as well as of the cognitive functions.

Passionate believer in reason as he was, he was also keenly aware of the shortcomings of reason. Yet he dwelt in a pre-Freudian innocence of the great non-rational forces of the mind. His psychology remains, to us, very naïve, although shrewdly observant within the limits of his age.

Not only was he pre-Freud but also pre-modern biology. If he had been familiar with the modern notion of organism, he would have avoided the crudity of his image of 'white paper or wax to be moulded'. R. H. Quick, in his *Essays on Educational Reformers* – still a classic after very nearly a hundred years – says: 'Perhaps the development of an organism was a conception that could not have been formed without a great advance in physical science. Froebel who makes most of it learnt it from the scientific study of trees and from mineralogy.'

Nevertheless, Locke's contribution to educational thinking had great virtues. He realized that the true starting-point of education is the child and his needs. He emphasizes the importance of *observing*

children, and of planning their education in the light of that observation. He knows that children reveal themselves when at play and
unaware of being observed, though he did not fully appreciate
that play has educative value in itself. He recognizes the need for
freedom, and for a proper balance between freedom and authority.
Freedom is needed because children must grow; they must play,
experiment, and make mistakes. The teacher must appeal to curiosity, and stimulate the desire to learn – otherwise no learning will
take place. Yet children must acquire disciplined habits, including
the acceptance of authority; strict authority is needed to prevent
wrong development. The balance of freedom and authority should
be proportionate to age and maturity; and to maintain a proper
balance is 'the true secret of education'.

Locke is entitled to be numbered among the originators of *child-
centred education*, although he sometimes did not see the remoter
implications of his own ideas.

Above all, he was a person of abundant common sense, humanity
and humour – eminently sane.

The main issues with which Locke is concerned in his philosophy
of education can perhaps be best seen in terms of certain tensions in
his thinking, some of which have already been observed. Locke
was a man of practical good sense, and could express himself
vividly and effectively. As a practical man, much involved in affairs
most of his life, he was more concerned with good sense than with
logical consistency. He is in some ways inconsistent, partly because
he represents a transition from one school of philosophy to another,
and partly because he uses overstatement to make his points clear.
His contradictions are more apparent than real, and can be re-
solved on the plane of practical wisdom. There are mainly four such
apparent contradictions, and they are closely related with one
another.

I. REASON AS AN INFALLIBLE GUIDE TO TRUTH

a] In the *Essay* and the *Conduct of Understanding* he relies heavily on
the guidance of reason. 'The faculty of reasoning seldom or never

deceives those who trust in it.' (*C. of U.*) And, in a letter to Molyneux, he expressed his belief that 'there are very few things of pure
speculation wherein two thinking men who impartially seek truth
can differ if they give themselves the leisure to examine their hypotheses and understand one another'. In this connexion it is worth
bearing in mind that his idea of religion was very intellectualistic.
Locke rightly believed – and in this he anticipated modern
authorities such as Dr Susan Isaacs – that children are responsive to
an appeal to reason at a much earlier age than was commonly
recognized, and he counsels patience and sympathy in reaching the
child's understanding at a reasoning level.

At the same time, his belief in reason led him to take too purely
cognitive a view of the whole business of learning. He treats the
imagination as a source of mischief, and has little use for music and
poetry. He pays little attention to the education of feeling, except
in so far as is implied in the priority of virtue in the education of the
whole man (in the *Thoughts*).

b] On the other hand, Locke recognizes that man is seldom rational.
In the *Conduct of the Understanding* he goes as far as to say that, if we
are seeking an example of a mind that can be sure of certainty, we
must go to 'angels and separate spirits who may be endowed with
more comprehensive faculties' than we possess. He lists the sources
of error in reasoning. The *Conduct of the Understanding* is largely
an essay on the causes of irrationality; and he has some very sound
practical advice to offer on how to minimize the risks of error.
Because the capacity of children to exercise reason is limited, they
must be educated largely by the formation of *habits*.

Locke's emphasis on habit-formation leads him at times to appear
as an apostle of stern discipline, in contrast with the almost indul-
gent attitude which he sometimes adopts towards the ways of
childhood. There is here, however, no real contradiction. Habit
was not, for Locke, a Procrustean bed or strait-jacket. It was not a
matter of unintelligent memorization and mechanical learning. He
did not use the word 'habit' in any pejorative sense, as we often do.
He meant much more what the modern social psychologist calls

'attitudes'. In Locke's view, habits must be acquired through the use of natural impulses (such as curiosity), and the child's willing and intelligent co-operation is necessary. As far as possible, live, first-hand experience should be present, not second-hand, predigested material. Truth must be seen with our own eyes.

There is much truth in Locke's insistence on the importance of habit. As Bacon says in his essay *Of Custom and Education*: 'Men's thoughts are much according to their inclination; their discourse and speeches according to their learning and infused opinions; but their deeds are often as they have been accustomed.' We change our opinions more easily than we change our behaviour.

Nevertheless, it is a valid criticism of Locke that his faith in habit was excessive. He thought, for example, that a child who eats enough bread will come to like it; and that by going to bed early and rising early young people will be accustomed to avoid the unhealthy and unsafe hours of debauchery. He never fully allows for the tendency of the young to react cussedly against their training, nor for the attractions of forbidden fruit.

2. THE PRIMACY OF INTELLECT. THE ROLE OF REASON IN THE FORMATION OF CHARACTER

a] In the *Conduct of the Understanding* Locke not only states his faith in reason as a guide to true knowledge but also as a director of action. He says that the will is subject to the understanding (echoing Socrates' 'To know the good is to do the good'). Although, for Locke, the will has 'supreme command' as an agent, the will itself 'never fails in its obedience to the dictates of the understanding'. It is interesting that, in his considerable concern about the right development of moral character, Locke makes very little reference to religious education. Moral training was to be done through discipline. The pupil must learn to 'deny himself his own desires, cross his inclinations, and purely follow what reason directs'.

b] In spite of this strong and uncompromising statement, Locke elsewhere recognizes that reason is distorted by feeling. He readily admits the limitations of reason when he says that it is much more difficult for a child to habituate himself to virtuous conduct than to

pursue academic studies successfully. In making this admission, he
was saying more than he realized.

In the *Thoughts*, the cultivation of the intellect loses its primacy,
and Locke shows instead a concern for the development of the whole
man, with these priorities: virtue, wisdom, manners, learning. The
subordination of the intellectual is partly due to the special purpose
of the *Thoughts* – the education of the gentleman – but by no means
wholly so. Although he does not demand that a gentleman should
be a scholar, Locke has no use for a gentleman who lets his mind run
to seed. And, quite apart from its special purpose, the *Thoughts* lay
valuable emphasis on the teacher's obligation to care more about
the kind of people that his pupils will *become* than about what they
will *know*.

3. TRUTH AN END IN ITSELF

a] Truth was for Locke (and in this he was an exception to the
ordinary run of mankind) an end in itself. And, by 'truth' he meant
primarily intellectual truth. He wrote to Bolde: 'Believe it, my
good friend, to love truth for truth's sake is the principal part of
human perfection in this world and the seed plot of all other virtues.' In this attitude he was a non-utilitarian.

b] In another sense Locke was very much a utilitarian, in that he
had no place for useless knowledge. In the *Thoughts* he emphasizes
the need for what is taught to be *usable*. His whole approach to
education in the *Thoughts* is pragmatic enough to satisfy the
modern pragmatists. He recommends that the sons of gentlemen
should learn a trade (though nobody took any notice of this), and
went to extremes of practicality in depreciating poetry and music.
The utilitarian spirit is clear in this passage from the *Thoughts*:
'Since it cannot be hoped he should have time and strength to learn
all things, most pains should be taken about what is most necessary,
and that principally looked after which will be of most and fre-
quentest use to him in the world.'

4. NATURE AND NURTURE

a] We have already seen that, in asking what is the essence of true knowledge (a main purpose in the *Essay*), Locke turned away from the Platonic–Aristotelian tradition, dominant in Oxford, by which philosophers had tried to derive knowledge from the operations of reason alone, and attacked the doctrine of 'innate ideas'. The source of knowledge, for Locke, was sense-experience; and he was one of the pioneers of the modern empirical approach.

In education, the empirical principle is apparent in Locke's emphasis on finding out for oneself. 'Knowing is seeing.' 'We cannot see through another man's eyes.' 'As much real knowledge as you can.'

Locke's emphasis on the importance of the senses was mainly as doorways through which knowledge entered the mind. He never went as far as Rousseau in valuing aesthetic experience and in urging the importance of doing rather than knowing. Although Locke's empirical theory of knowledge was implicitly the one that science uses to explore the world, his educational application of it was almost wholly passive. Learning for him was receptive rather than active; and in this respect he was not in line with modern educational thought.

Locke's concern to stress the importance of experience in education led him to overstatement in the well-known passage which likens the child's mind to 'white paper or wax to be moulded'. In the *Thoughts* he says: 'The difference to be found in the manners and abilities of men is owing more to their education than to anything else.' But he did not go as far as Helvetius (1715–71): 'L'Education peut tout.' Helvetius denied *any* inherent faculties and held that man is nothing but the product of his education.

The unfortunate mechanical image reminds us that Locke was not in a position to think in terms of a growing organism. Froebel and Pestalozzi said later what Locke might have said if science had been further advanced in his time. There is a truer perspective in this remark by Comenius (whose writings Locke, incidentally, had read): 'Nature has implanted within us the seeds of learning, of virtue, and of piety. The object of education is to bring these seeds to perfection.'

b] In apparent contradiction to his assertion that the differences between men are due more to their education than to anything else, Locke says (in the *Thoughts*): 'God has stamped certain characters upon men's minds, which, like their shape, may perhaps be a little mended, but can hardly be totally altered.' 'But of this be sure, after all is done, the bias will always hang on that side nature first placed it.'

Notwithstanding the unfortunate image of the *tabula rasa*, Locke elsewhere makes it quite clear that he recognizes the importance of natural endowment. In this context he urges the importance of observing children as individuals, especially watching them at play when their natures will be revealed. In the *Conduct of the Understanding* he explicitly recognizes that there is 'great inequality of parts' among 'men of equal education'.

In order to see Locke's work in its proper perspective, it is desirable to ask what earlier writers influenced him, and what influence he had on those who came after.

The first question is not easy to answer. Locke makes little explicit acknowledgement, and much of the influence upon him must have been in the intellectual climate of his time. His educational thinking, however, was certainly influenced by Montaigne (1533–92), whom he is known to have read, and by Comenius (1592–1670). He probably had read Comenius, and may also have read Rabelais, who influenced Montaigne and emphasized the importance of first-hand knowledge. Comenius, in his *Didactica Magna*, had proclaimed the principle that everything should be taught through the medium of the senses. He criticized the teaching of physics in his day because it consisted merely in reading Aristotle. He was equally modern in his view that the experience of things should come before the names of things, and practical examples before generalized rules. Montaigne had shown that Latin could be learnt conversationally as easily as one's mother tongue. Comenius took the same view. And Locke reflected the opinions of both. Comenius himself had been greatly influenced by Francis Bacon's empirical method. It is clear, therefore, that Locke, though he gave a new impulse to empiricism, by no means originated it.

Locke's influence was greater on the Continent than in this country. He certainly influenced Helvetius who carried empiricism to an extreme. It has already been noted that Helvetius took the *tabula rasa* theory to the length of 'L'Education peut tout'. For him, Locke's 'powers of the mind' were themselves the result of sensations.

The influence of both Comenius' and Locke's emphasis on education through sense-experience is clearly seen in Rousseau. The influence of Locke's views on Rousseau's *Émile* is obvious. Both writers emphasized the importance of family life, of bodily exercise, and of first-hand experience through the senses as against book-knowledge. Both held that education should be based on a careful study of the child, his nature and needs. Both envisaged the care of an individual pupil by a tutor; Émile was to be handed over to 'un homme de génie'.

But it would be a mistake to overestimate Locke's influence on Rousseau. There are important differences. Locke never made Rousseau's basic assumption of an ideal State of Nature, which had progressively degenerated through a historical process which must be reversed. Locke, in his reaction against bookishness, never went as far as Rousseau, who held that the educator should teach nothing for the first twelve years of the child's life. Nor did Locke, whose notion of learning, with its image of the *tabula rasa*, remained passive rather than active, ever reach Rousseau's idea of education as an uninhibited unfolding of the child's nature. In Locke's system, especially on the side of moral education, there remained a strong authoritarian element. Rousseau's lead was followed by Pestalozzi and Froebel, who saw the aim of education as the natural development of the child's innate capacities.

It is interesting to note that Locke's *tabula rasa* could supply a doctrine for political revolution, and has in fact done so. If all men are equal, and their differences are the result of environment, including education, then the ideal community can be produced by

E

applying the right social influences. This doctrine can be traced in the French and American Revolutions (which proclaimed that men are created equal), and more recently in the totalitarian countries (educational policy in the U.S.S.R. has always been reluctant to acknowledge the natural differences between human beings). Rousseau, however, took the other line of preaching revolution as a rejection of historic social injustice and a Return to Nature.

Neither Comenius, Locke, nor Rousseau gave much guidance on the practical methodology of learning. It remained for Pestalozzi (1746–1827), Herbart (1776–1841), and Froebel (1782–1852) to pioneer in this field. For example, although Locke recommended children's games as a pleasant camouflage for instruction, and as a means of studying the nature of children, it was Froebel who realized that play is in itself educative.

Some of Locke's more revolutionary suggestions not unnaturally fell on barren soil. No one took any notice of his suggestion that a gentleman's son should learn a trade. In his day the 'stereotype of the leisured class' still prevailed, and people did not yet appreciate the social revolution that had been going on in English life since the rise of the bourgeois middle class with the growth of trade in the sixteenth and seventeenth centuries. The English social system has always been an inspired mixture of fact and fiction; that is perhaps the secret of its tough tenacity.

At the other end of the social scale, Locke's suggestion of 'working schools' for the children of the labouring classes (their instruction to be paid for from the produce of their work) never came to anything, except that it may have influenced the 'Charity School' movement of the eighteenth century, sponsored by the S.P.C.K. and S.P.G. The Charity Schools, however, taught enough of the Three R's to fit a child for apprenticeship, and thus went beyond Locke's proposal.

Locke himself was of his time in taking no interest in the possibility of educational provision by the State, although in seventeenth-century England some Puritans advocated State education – an idea that was carried across the Atlantic by emigrants and put into practice in the New England Colonies. In England, State education had to wait till the nineteenth century. Locke was the less likely to be interested in State schools because he had little use for schools of any kind. Those of us who take for granted not only the provision of schools by the State but the statutory requirement that children should be educated, may recall that, only a century ago, Herbert Spencer expressed the view that compulsion of parents to educate their children was an unwarrantable interference with individual liberty.

It is customary to emphasize the limited objective of Locke's *Thoughts Concerning Education*. It is true that he was concerned specifically with the education of sons of gentlemen ('how a young gentleman should be brought up from his infancy'), that he has practically nothing to say about the education of girls, and that he had no use for the schools of his day, recommending instead the employment of a private tutor.

Even if he had taken a broader assignment, however, it is doubtful whether Locke's views on the aims and methods of education would have been substantially different. It is often said that the role of the intellect is played up in the *Conduct of the Understanding*, and played down in the *Thoughts*. To some extent this is so; but the reason is not merely that the sons of gentlemen did not need to be scholars.

The whole purpose of Locke's writings on the human understanding was to examine the cognitive processes. When he turned to the business of educating human beings, he took for granted that a person is a good deal more than an intellect. He is not anti-intellectual in his views on the education of young gentlemen; in fact, he had some hard things to say about gentlemen who neglect the things of the mind for excessive indulgence in sport and drinking. But he is sane enough to see that the object of study is 'an increase of the powers and activity of the mind, not an enlargement of its possessions'. The implied condemnation of mere memorization is in fact a criticism of the schools of the time, where too often the schoolmaster's 'knowledge' made no demand on the reasoning faculty. Locke's criterion of knowledge was much more rigorous than that of most schoolmasters.

Locke, who had not enjoyed his own schooldays, was much aware of the imperfections of the schools of his time. Not only was rote-learning emphasized at the expense of thought and understanding (and Latin grammar at the expense of a practical mastery of the native tongue); but the boarding-schools were rough and undisciplined.

There is no doubt that the schools of that time were very bad. That good scholars and good men emerged from the system is chiefly evidence of the power of the human mind and spirit to survive the worst that education can inflict.

Little or no attempt was made to educate character (the great preoccupation of the public schools two centuries later). Academically, the Renaissance and Reformation, for a time at least, brought a *narrowing* of curriculum by concentrating on Latin and Greek instead of the old Trivium (grammar, logic, rhetoric) and Quadrivium (arithmetic, geometry, music, astronomy). Nor were these languages even taught well. Milton, in the *Tractate*, commented: 'We do amiss to spend seven or eight years merely in scraping together so much miserable Latin and Greek as might be learnt otherwise easily and delightfully in one year.' Locke's comment on the study of the classics in his time was: 'We learnt not to live but to dispute.'

There is no reason to think that Locke was unfair to the schools of his day. And it is interesting to note that Canon Evan Daniel, whose edition of the *Thoughts* was published in 1880, says that the teaching in the public schools remained more or less unchanged until about 1860.

Teaching was not a reputable profession in the seventeenth century. Men took to it only as a *pis-aller* or used it as a stepping stone. There was little or no systematic study of education or of children. To say that Locke was an amateur in the field of education is no condemnation in the context of historical perspective. What is more to the point is that he was a keen and shrewd observer, with a natural liking for children, and much practical wisdom. He was over sixty when he wrote the *Thoughts*, and had seen a good deal of the world.

Considering that Locke was a bachelor, and had little direct experience of teaching children,[2] Locke's views on children and their education were remarkably realistic and sagacious. His apparent Puritan severity[3] was a salutary reaction against the over-indulgence of which too many well-to-do parents were guilty – alternating with vindictiveness when they saw the unlovely consequences of their unwisdom. And Locke would have something to say to the modern parent in the affluent society whose offspring increasingly blackmail him into giving them what 'all the others have got'.[4]

But Locke is careful to counsel against excessive punishment, which will make children hate the tasks with which it is associated, and inhibit their learning capacity. (Children cannot learn 'whilst their thoughts are possessed and disturbed with any passion, especially fear'. Children will learn three times as much when 'in tune'.) Children must be tenderly used, and must play and have playthings.

If Locke appears to rely overmuch on habit-formation (the child who eats enough bread will come to like it), it must be remembered that he saw the fallacy of coercion. Coerce a child to spin a top and he will dislike it – which reminds us of the well-known story of "Ow I 'ate my 'obby!'

In general, Locke's methods are eminently sane. Example and practice are better than precept. Children should not be wearied with lectures. They are capable of reasoning within limits. They are not 'capable of reasonings from remote principles. They cannot conceive the force of long deductions.' 'The reasons that move them must be obvious and level to their thoughts, and such as may (if I may so say) be felt and touched.' They should be as far as possible taken into confidence and dealt with as one human being to another. Above all, there is need for honesty in the teacher; children 'easily perceive when they are slighted or deceived'.

'He that has found a way, how to keep up a child's spirit, easy, active, and free; and yet at the same time to restrain him from many things that are uneasy to him; he, I say, that knows how to reconcile these seeming contradictions has, in my opinion, got the true secret of education.'

6 · English Educational Thought and Practice Before Locke

'Good Lord! how many good and clear wits of children be now-adays perished by ignorant schoolmasters!' So wrote Sir Thomas Elyot in the *Governour* (1531), a book which, significantly, was written in English and not in Latin.

Enough has been said in the previous chapter to show that English education in Locke's time left much to be desired, and also that Locke, for all his sound sense, has no great claim to originality as an educational thinker.

In order to see Locke's thought in its proper perspective it is necessary to take a more careful look at what had been going on in English educational thought and practice during the century or so before his time. This can perhaps be most conveniently done by examining three propositions: (*a*) In certain ways the effects of the Renaissance and Reformation upon education had not been good; (*b*) at the same time, and gathering momentum in the seventeenth century, there was an important forward movement in educational thought; (*c*) educational practice, though certainly influenced for the better during the century before Locke, was very slow to respond to the reforming zeal of Locke and many before him.

a] The influence of the Renaissance and Reformation on education was by no means entirely beneficial.

Reference has already been made to the fact that, academically, the Renaissance brought a narrowing of the curriculum by a new concentration on Latin and Greek (the Trivium of grammar, logic, and rhetoric) to the disadvantage of the subjects of the old Quadrivium (arithmetic, geometry, music, astronomy). Moreover, the enthusiasm of the Renaissance scholars for all things classical tended to enhance the backward-looking glorification of the past which had for centuries been part of our educational tradition.

The schools themselves suffered a serious blow in the Reformation by the dissolution of the chantries (chapels endowed to say masses for the dead). Many of the chantries had schools attached to them, mostly giving secondary education. Nearly half these schools gradually perished when the Crown (Henry VIII and Edward VI) seized the chantry endowments. It is true that the chantries were compensated by fixed payments. But the value of these depreciated. The important fact is that the landed endowments were confiscated. Most of Edward VI's scholastic 'foundations' were schools that were allowed to survive. So far from being a creditable achievement, the educational policy of Henry VIII and Edward VI was a lamentably lost opportunity. The historian G. M. Trevelyan says that, if even half the endowments of the chantries had been devoted to education, England would have had the best secondary education in Europe. Trevelyan's view is probably an overstatement, and does not take sufficient account of the poor standards of teaching and defective methods; but there is enough truth in it to correct the traditional popular view of educational progress in the mid-sixteenth century.

English education was badly hit by the Clarendon Code at the time of the Restoration of 1660, as was seen in an earlier chapter. The Five Mile Act forbade any schoolmaster who was not by oath an Anglican to come within five miles of a corporate town. It is true that, even within a few years, the enforcement of these laws was somewhat eased. But it is equally certain that the whole effect of the organized persecution of dissenters was to discourage and exclude some of the most progressive educational thought and experiment of the time. One of the consequences of this proscription of dissenters was the development, under their own steam and outside the Establishment, of the Dissenting Academies, certainly the most modern schools and colleges of the seventeenth and eighteenth centuries. Forced out of the main stream of educational development, these Academies had little influence on English education in general, at least until the nineteenth century.

b] Perhaps the most important long-term outcome of the Renaissance was the modern spirit of scientific inquiry. In education the new spirit meant a profoundly significant change of perspective, away from rote-learning and formalism to practical use, and from the authority of tradition to discovery.

The change was revolutionary in all fields of thought. The scholars of the earlier Renaissance had looked back to a Golden Age of classical perfection. By the beginning of the seventeenth century, thinkers were looking forward, especially in their inquiry into man's place in Nature. The new spirit of discovery, active geographically in the fifteenth century, was invading the world of the mind by the time of William Harvey (1578–1657), who discovered the circulation of the blood, Isaac Newton (1642–1727), whose work on light, gravitation, and the calculus gave him a pre-eminent place among the great names of science, Gottfried Leibnitz (1646–1716), who devised the infinitesimal calculus, and many others.

The personification of the new age was perhaps Francis Bacon (1561–1626) who pointed out the two 'distempers of learning': the emptiness of mere verbalism, and the futility of theory unrelated to observed fact. Applying Bacon's principles to the schools, Comenius (1592–1670) said: 'I beseech you let this be our business that the schools may cease to *persuade* and begin to *demonstrate*; cease to *dispute* and begin to *look*; cease lastly to *believe* and begin to *know*.'

The causes of great historical changes are never easy to disentangle; and the emergence of the modern scientific spirit in Europe at that time remains something of a mystery. We can, however, observe certain significant connexions. For example, it can be no accident that the development of modern physical science followed the change in painting and sculpture which was marked by an altogether new interest in accurate observation, including anatomy and perspective. Nor can the growth of science be unconnected with the Protestant swing of emphasis away from the acceptance of traditional authority to a personal responsibility for seeking the truth at its sources and doing one's own thinking. At a more practical level, there is a clear connexion between the growth of science and the growth of trade and commerce. Trade, navigation, and the extension of international relations, needed educated men of action, who knew some mathematics and science, history, geography, and modern languages. T. L. Jarman, in his *Landmarks in the History of Education*, quotes some interesting figures[1] for the intended careers of students in Dissenting Academies. It is true that the figures are for a century after Locke; but the trend is significant. A century *before* Locke's time, almost the whole grammar school population would have been aiming professionally at divinity, medicine, and law. The figures for Warrington Academy in the mid-eighteenth century show that 25 per cent were aiming at commerce, 12 per cent at divinity, and about 6 per cent each at medicine and law. The rest are unspecified.

There was, then, a considerable wind of change in the mental climate of the seventeenth century, which produced a good deal of new thinking about education. John Colet, the friend of Erasmus and re-founder of St Paul's School, protested against the needless complication of grammar-teaching a century before Locke. 'For in the beginning men spake not Latin because such rules were made, but, contrariwise, because men spake such Latin, upon that followed the rules, and were made. That is to say, Latin speech was before the rules, and not the rules before Latin speech.'

One of the changes for the better that had taken place in the schools before Locke's time was this simplification of grammar. Lily, the first High Master of St Paul's, was the author of a new Latin grammar which was ordered, by Henry VIII, Edward VI, and Elizabeth, to be used in schools. Lily's grammar replaced Donatus, the standard medieval textbook.

Notwithstanding this simplification of grammar, the teaching continued very formal for a long time to come. A boy's time in school was still mainly occupied with Latin, and it was not unusual for the speaking of Latin to be enforced in play hours. The habit continued of making boys learn grammar *before* reading any of the literature, and Lily's grammar was being learnt by heart even after

1700. Learning grammar by heart was supplemented by the exercise, unchanged since the twelfth century, of disputing about the principles of grammar. Stowe, writing in 1603, says that 'the arguing of the schoolboys about the principles of grammar hath been continued even till our time'.

If no substantial reform of educational practice had taken place before Locke's time, the same cannot be said of educational thought. Most of what Locke had to say had in fact been said during the hundred years before he published his book.

The first English writer whose work has survived as a classic, and exerted influence abroad, was Roger Ascham (1515–68), who wrote *The Scholemaster* (posthumously published, 1570). Whether he deserves his fame is open to question; but at least he broke new ground in the methodology of Latin teaching. He advised the translation of Cicero, Livy, and Caesar 'into plain natural English', and advocated the method of double translation, by which a passage from a Latin author was put into English, then back into Latin, and the pupil's Latin version compared with the original. Ascham protested against the excessive tyranny of formal grammar, and refers (whether with a sycophantic tongue in his loyal cheek we cannot tell) to 'our most noble Queen Elizabeth, who never took yet Greek or Latin grammar in her hand after the first declining of a noun and a verb; but . . . hath attained to such a perfect understanding in both the tongues and to such a ready utterance of the Latin, and that with such a judgment, as there be few now in both Universities or elsewhere in England that be in both tongues comparable with Her Majesty.' Nevertheless, Ascham's precise directions for teaching remain, on the whole, fairly heavily weighted on the formal, grammatical side.

Richard Mulcaster (1531–1611), author of *Positions* and *Elementarie*, was a practising schoolmaster, and a famous one, being the first headmaster of Merchant Taylors'. Hampered by a complicated style and much personal vanity, he has the great merit of having urged some very modern reforms. His progressive views are the more remarkable in one who was constantly involved in the practical work of teaching.

He is probably the first English writer to propose a system of training colleges for teachers; and we had to wait the best part of three hundred years to see a training college established.

He urged the importance of studying and gaining a mastery of the mother-tongue. In this connexion it is worth noting the great impact on English education of Shakespeare, Spenser, and – much more important – the Authorized Version of the Bible. The availability of the Bible in English, by the end of the sixteenth century, is one of the great events of English history; its language and its substance did much to shape the minds and characters of generations of Englishmen. Read a life of Oliver Cromwell, and try to imagine how he would have thought, spoken, and acted without the Bible. As there came to be a substantial body of contemporary English literature, scholars wrote in English rather than in Latin, and the schools paid more attention to English. Milton learnt to love the English language as a boy at St Paul's, though in his generation there was still little enough time to spare in school from Latin, Greek, and Hebrew.

Mulcaster believed in the all-round development of mind and body, and did not hold with excessive pressure on the intelligent learners; he would have raised his voice against cramming for the G.C.E. Like Montaigne, he maintained that the learner, not the thing to be learnt, should be central in education. He spoke up for the education of girls (which Locke virtually ignores). And he makes the very modern suggestion (which would even today make headlines in the educational press) that those who teach the youngest children should have the smallest classes and the highest pay.

Charles Hoole, who was headmaster of two schools, published several books in the middle of the seventeenth century, in which he complains of the neglect of English in the schools, and also refers to Comenius' principle that observation should come before instruction; we should not teach 'children as we do parrots to speak they know not what'.

Sir William Petty in 1647 addressed an *Epistle* to Master Samuel Hartlib, urging that children should be introduced to *things* rather than to 'a rabble of words'. 'For we see children do delight in drums, pipes, fiddles, guns made of elder sticks, and bellows' noses, piped keys, etc., painting flags and ensigns with elderberries and corn-poppy, making ships with paper, and setting even nutshells a-swimming, handling the tools of workmen as soon as they turn their backs . . .'

c] Enough examples have been given to show that, by Locke's time, there was a clear trend of opinion in education towards prac-tical activity and discovery and away from the traditional verbalism and learning by rote. Some of the writers quoted were themselves schoolmasters, and there is evidence of some advance in educational practice; the adoption of Lily's grammar is an example.

In general, however, the new ideas had made little impact on the schools, even by 1700. Educational progress is always slow; and one must remember that it is never easy for practising teachers to make radical reforms. They have to come to terms with the reali-ties of the classroom, including limited supplies of old-fashioned books, inconveniently large classes, and – an important element – the rooted conservatism of boys themselves. To these difficulties must be added the fact that the teachers, if they have been trained at all, have been trained in the atmosphere of the past, and in any case will think most easily in terms of their own upbringing. Few practising teachers have time or inclination to be visionaries; they have to plod through the days and weeks as they come.

The schools went on much as they had been, and for many more generations after Locke. John Dury, a contemporary of Locke's, in *The Reformed School* (about 1650) voiced the general complaint that children were set to learn words and sentences without under-standing them. And Sir William Petty, already mentioned, wrote: 'Since few children have need of reading before they know or can be acquainted with the things they read of; or of writing before their thoughts are worth the recording . . . our opinion is that those things being withal somewhat above their capacity . . . be deferred awhile, and others more needful for them, such as are in the order of Nature . . . be studied before them. We wish, there-fore, that the educands be taught to observe and remember all sensible objects and actions . . . which the educators must upon all occasions expound unto them.'

John Milton, in his famous *Tractate*, has a foot in the two camps of past and future. His doctrine is liberal. '. . . because our understanding cannot in this body found itself but on sensible things, nor arrive so clearly to the knowledge of God and things invisible, as by conning over the visible and inferior creature, the same method is necessarily to be followed in all discreet teaching . . . language is but the instrument conveying to us things useful to be known. And though a linguist should pride himself to have all the tongues that Babel cleft the world into, yet, if he have not studied the solid things in them as well as the words and lexicons, he were nothing so much to be esteemed a learned man as any yeoman or tradesman competently wise in his mother-dialect only.'

Milton proposed, for every city in England, a joint school and university for 120 boarders. Otherwise, when it comes to curriculum and method, Milton's prescriptions are disappointing. His curriculum is grossly overloaded, and remains very bookish, consisting mainly of Latin, Greek, and Hebrew. It is true that he suggested some history, geography, and natural science; but it is not easy to see how they could be fitted in.

It is very unlikely that Milton's opinions on education would have survived if they had been written by anyone else. They have been carried down to posterity on the tide of his immortal prose, which, like the language of Abraham Lincoln or Winston Churchill, has the power of ennobling the stature of common things.

Milton's statements of the nature and purpose of education are well known. 'I call therefore a complete and generous education, that which fits a man to perform justly, skilfully, and magnanimously all the offices both private and public of peace and war.' 'The end then of learning is to repair the ruins of our first parents by regaining to know God aright, and out of that knowledge to love Him, to imitate Him, to be like Him, as we may the nearest by possessing our souls of true virtue, which being united to the heavenly grace of faith, makes up the highest perfection.'

Less well known are his remarks on speech. 'For me Englishmen being far northerly, do not open our mouths in the cold air, wide enough to grace a Southern tongue; but are observed by all other nations to speak exceeding close and inward: so that to smatter Latin with an English mouth, is as ill a hearing as Law-French.'

By Locke's time, then, the *idea* of educational reform was in the air, though it was very slow to come into practice. The most important practical demonstration of the new thinking was in the Dissenting Academies, of which something has been said elsewhere.

Although Locke's views on education were on the whole no original, he writes clearly and effectively, with astringent humour. His book had considerable influence abroad, partly no doubt because he had friends in France and the Netherlands and had spent some years of his life in those countries.

One final comment is worth making on the educational thought of the seventeenth century. Nobody, as yet, saw education as something to which all human beings had a natural right. Although Locke suggested trade schools, these would not have offered anything that we would have recognized as a liberal education. Academic education, in those days, was for the few.

We must remember, however, that, in pre-industrial times, most young people could learn what they needed – not only to earn a living but to live as responsible members of a community – though growing up in the society in which they were born. Apprenticeship still operated usefully. The Churches were a real part of life. The gentry and nobility had their own system of social education (lads of good family often resided in a noble household as apprentices boarded with their masters). In fact the community as such educated the next generation to a far greater extent than is possible today. It was the Industrial Revolution which made it necessary for everyone to go to school. For, in an industrialized society, people must be able to read, write, and count. The coming of political democracy made it necessary for the schools to attempt something more than the three Rs. The social revolution and cultural disintegration of the present century piled still heavier burdens on the schools, which can no longer operate within a generally accepted framework of beliefs and standards, but have to help the young to rediscover the meaning and purpose of life. Locke, and his generation, would have been astonished to read, in the Education Act of 1944, not only that schools must be provided for all children but that the public system of education was responsible for the 'spiritual, moral, mental, and physical development of the community'.

PART THREE

Locke's 'Thoughts Concerning Education'

The third part of this book consists of an analysis, by quotation and comment, of Locke's book, Thoughts Concerning Education.

As has been already observed, Locke's book originated in letters written to Edward Clarke. Even when published as a book it retained some of the desultory character to be expected of a collection of letters. To take a single example, his views on the power of education as a moulding force are scattered in paragraphs as far apart as 1, 2, 32, 216.

While keeping the paragraph numbering, which is Locke's own, I have rearranged the material in three main sections: first, the general principles of education; secondly, the care of the child, including bodily health, parents' treatment of their children, and the qualities of a good tutor; thirdly, the curriculum or programme of studies.

The edition used here is R. H. Quirk's, based on the first collected edition of Locke's Works, published in 1714. This is the one used by F. W. Garforth in his edition of the Thoughts *(Heinemann, 1964). The American Professor Peter Gay, in his* John Locke on Education *(Teachers College, Columbia, Classics in Education, No. 20, 1964) uses the 1823 edition of* The Works of John Locke. *There is little significant difference between the two editions, though a few paragraphs are differently numbered. Both Mr Garforth's and Professor Gay's books are edited texts, with fairly brief introductions.*

7 · General Principles of Education

I. NATURE AND NURTURE

Locke's belief in the power of education is clearly expressed. 'The difference to be found in the manners and abilities of men is owing more to their education than to anything else.' (32) '. . . of all the men we meet with, nine parts of ten are what they are, good or evil, useful or not, by their education . . .' (1) 'I imagine the minds of children as easily turned this or that way as water itself . . .' (2) He considers the minds of young children 'only as white paper, or wax, to be moulded and fashioned as one pleases'. (216)

Although in these remarks, scattered through the book, Locke may seem to genuflect at the altar of environmental pressure as abjectly as any modern anthropologist, he is too shrewd to be taken in by his own rather unfortunate similes. Locke is often guilty of overstatement, in order to make a point; and without his over-statements his book would be less readable. But in the long run the ship of his common sense keeps a pretty even keel.

What he says about the potency of education is balanced by his recognition of the importance of the individual's innate qualities. With his usual flair for analogy he observes that the native material, on which the impressions of experience are made, varies from one person to another. 'There are not more differences in men's faces, and the outward lineaments of their bodies, than there are in the makes and tempers of their minds; only there is this difference, that the distinguishing characters of the face, and the lineaments of the body, grow more plain and visible with time and age; but the peculiar physiognomy of the mind is most discernible in children, before art and cunning hath taught them to hide their deformities, and conceal their ill inclinations, under a dissembled outside.' (*101*) '. . . it will be fit to consider which way the natural make of his mind inclines him. Some men by the unalterable frame of their constitutions are stout, others timorous, some confident, others modest, tractable or obstinate, curious or careless, quick or slow.' (*101*) 'Begin therefore betimes nicely to observe your son's temper . . . These native propensities . . . are not to be cured by rules or direct contest . . . though with art they may be much mended and turned to good purposes. But . . . after all is done, the bias will always hang on that side nature first placed it.' (*102*) Of the 'various tempers, different inclinations' of children he says: 'The variety is so great that it would require a volume; nor would that reach it. Each man's mind has some peculiarity, as well as his face, that distinguishes him from all others; and there are possibly scarce two children who can be conducted by exactly the same method.' (*216*) 'God hath stamped certain characters upon men's minds, which, like their shapes, may perhaps be a little mended but can hardly be totally altered and transformed into the contrary.' (*66*)

The great educative agency is *habit*, and habit-formation should begin early. 'What you think necessary for them to do, settle in them by an indispensable practice as often as the occasion returns . . . *This will beget habits in them*, which, being once established, operate of themselves easily and naturally without the assistance of the memory.' (*66*) Of the value of discipline and the disciplined life Locke says: 'The great principle and foundation of all virtue and worth is placed in this: that a man is able to deny himself his own desires, cross his own inclinations and purely follow what reason directs as best, though the appetite lean the other way.' (*33*). 'It seems plain to me that the principle of all virtue and excellency lies in a power of denying ourselves the satisfaction of our own desires, where reason does not authorize them. This power is to be got and improved by custom, made easy and familiar by early practice . . . I would advise that, contrary to the ordinary way, children should be used to submit their desires and go without their longings even from their very cradles. The first thing they should learn to know should be that they were not to have anything because it pleased them, but because it was thought fit for them.' (*38*) 'Would you have your son obedient to you when past a child, be sure then to establish the authority of a father as soon as he is capable of submission and can understand in whose power he is. If you would have him stand in awe of you, imprint it in his infancy; and as he approaches more to a man, admit him nearer to your familiarity.' (*40*)

What Locke has to say about self-discipline and reasonable self-denial is salutary, and may be taken to heart in our own day. What he does not sufficiently recognize, perhaps, though he assuredly knew it, is the need for an overriding purpose or ideal in living that can effectively inspire self-discipline. Immediate pleasures can be sacrificed for the sake of greater and more lasting goods. St Paul's comparison of the Christian life with the training of an athlete is well known. But the athlete will not give up cigarettes and beer if there are no races to train for.

On the subject of habit, we may compare Locke's views with the modern social psychologist's emphasis on attitudes. There is a good deal of evidence, from modern research, to show that attitudes, emotional and largely social in their origin, have a good deal more to do with our behaviour than conscious thinking.

Here again, however, we may observe that Locke does not sufficiently acknowledge the importance of motivation in the formation of attitudes. The mere repetition of actions will not establish them as habitual. At the simplest, Pavlov, level there must be a bait – a positive motive.

2. THE HIERARCHY OF VALUES IN THE EDUCATION OF A GENTLEMAN

Locke thought that, if the leaders of society were educated, the health of society would follow. He wrote to Edward Clarke: 'If those of that rank are by their education once set right, they will quickly bring all the rest into order.' One can but speculate on what Locke would have thought of a social order in which trend-setting is so differently located that even the Tory party has to refashion its image so as to avoid appearing gentlemanly. The fact that Locke was advising on the education of a certain social group at a certain time in history does not, however, take away from the value of his scale of priorities in education.

Nor do the differences between Locke's world and our own mean that there is no longer any need for cultural leadership. It may, indeed, be argued that any kind of society that we can imagine needs cultural leadership located somewhere; and that one of our difficulties today is that the traditional leadership has broken down and nothing effective has been put in its place. It is agreed that, in the modern world, cultural leadership can no longer be located in a social class. Where, then, can it be located? Who should be the guardians of standards and values? The proprietors and operators of the mass media? The institutions of higher education? Or is it possible that the institutions of higher education could gain enough control of the mass media to use them for worthy educative purposes? There are hopeful signs, in the last ten years, that the universities are at length taking some interest both in the mass media and in their general responsibility towards the general public. But the weakness of the institutions of higher education as guardians of cultural values is partly that they have not enough power (i.e. money), and partly that, compared with a hereditary social class, they have no continuity. We have here a very difficult problem, and the future of our civilization is to no small extent bound up with our success or failure in solving it.

Locke states his educational aims thus. 'That which every gentleman . . . desires for his son, besides the estate he leaves him, is contained, I suppose, in these four things, virtue, wisdom, breeding and learning.' (*134*)

('I place *virtue* as the first and most necessary.' (*135*) 'As the foundation of this there ought very early to be imprinted on his mind a true notion of God . . . And consequent to this, instil into him a love and reverence of this Supreme Being' (*136*) It is interesting to note that there is very little reference to religion in the *Thoughts Concerning Education*. Locke's notion of religion was mainly intellectual and, although he regarded religion as the source and sanction of morality, religion for him seems to have had little inspirational connexion with the education of moral character and conduct. Truthfulness and consideration for others are qualities to be cultivated. 'Let him know that twenty faults are sooner to be forgiven than the straining of truth to cover anyone by an excuse.' (*139*) 'And to teach him betimes to love and be good-natured to others is to lay early the true foundation of an honest man; all injustice generally springing from too great love of ourselves and too little of others.' (*139*)

'*Wisdom* I take in the popular acceptation for a man's managing his business ably and with foresight in the world.' (*140*) Because this practical wisdom involves experience, it is 'above the reach of children'. But 'the greatest thing that in them can be done towards it is to hinder them as much as may be from cunning, which, being the ape of wisdom, is the most distant from it that can be'. (*140*)

Locke has much to say about *Good Breeding*, including manners. 'There are two sorts of ill breeding, the one a sheepish bashfulness, and the other a misbecoming negligence and disrespect in our carriage; both of which are avoided by duly observing this one rule, not to think meanly of ourselves and not to think meanly of others.' (*141*) 'The first part of this rule must not be understood in opposition to humility but to assurance.' (*142*) Among the faults that are opposite to civility he lists: natural roughness, contempt, censoriousness, captiousness, excess of ceremony, and forwardness to interrupt. 'There cannot be a greater rudeness than to interrupt another in the current of his discourse.' (*144*) He stresses the importance of being accustomed to the company of people who inspire respect; and also of inwardness rather than outwardness. 'And in good earnest, if I were to speak my mind freely, so children do nothing out of obstinacy, pride and ill nature, 'tis no great matter how they put off their hats or make legs.' (*145*) The refinements of behaviour will come later.

'You will wonder, perhaps, that I put *Learning* last, especially if I tell you I think it the least part. This may seem strange in the mouth of a bookish man.' (*147*) He recognizes the need for a gentleman to be able to read and write, and to express himself in his own language. Beyond that, Latin and Greek can be much overrated. 'I imagine you would think him a very foolish fellow that shall not value a virtuous or a wise man infinitely before a great scholar.' (*147*) We must remember that Locke's opinions of the value of academic studies were very much influenced by the poor state of classical teaching at that time. It was excessively formal, brought little understanding of the classical civilizations, and was a great waste of time.

In connexion with Locke's hierarchy of values in education, it is worth remembering that, in our own day, we still overweight education on the intellectual and academic side, especially in the upper reaches of the educational system. We should agree, in principle, that, in a well-educated man, there should be a proper balance between the elements of knowledge, skill, and feeling (the latter including moral as well as aesthetic feeling). Yet it is open to question how far we succeed in maintaining such a balance in the different stages of education. The primary school probably does best in this respect. In the university, and in the grammar school, the emphasis is heavily on the intellectual side. The reasons for this emphasis, in an age when more and more highly trained experts are wanted, and when places in higher education are being hotly com- peted for, are obvious enough. But is a lop-sided education a good education? We ought to ask ourselves whether, at the university level, we are educating human beings or only trying to train in- tellects. Are our young graduates as mature morally, aesthetically, as they are academically? Have they contemplated goodness and beauty as seriously as they have pursued truth? In our efforts to organize the education of the intellect, are we leaving the education of the rest of the personality to chance?

3. CHARACTER

'As the strength of the body lies chiefly in being able to endure hardships, so also does that of the mind.' (*33*) Locke's belief in self- denial and in control by reason has already been illustrated. It is interesting to note some of the faults of character which must be combated by education. Although Locke doubted the doctrine of

Original Sin, he certainly did not believe that children are naturally good. As to the method of education, he wisely prescribes example and practice rather than 'lectures'. (*67*) His list of faults include the following: '*Love of power and dominion.*' (*103*) Locke advises that the child should 'never be suffered to have what he craves, much less what he cries for'. (*106*) He explains that this does not mean that children should not express their proper needs, such as: 'I am hungry' or 'I am cold'. In genuine cases, ''tis the duty of their parents and those about them to relieve them'. (*106*) '*Crying* is a fault that should not be tolerated in children; not only for the unpleasant and unbecoming noise it fills the house with, but for more considerable reasons in reference to the children themselves.' (*111*) Two sorts of crying are distinguished: 'stubborn and domineering' and 'querulous and whining'. (*111*) For stubborn crying Locke discourages the frequent use of blows, for there is no use in beating children unless you subdue their minds. 'Without this, the beating of children is but a passionate tyranny over them; and it is mere cruelty, and not correction, to put their bodies in pain without doing their minds any good.' (*112*) When children cry from being hurt, compassion should be shown, but not too much. A breezy attitude to knocks and falls is advised; and the sufferer's thoughts should be diverted when possible.

Cowardice. Courage is largely innate; but a good deal can be done to cultivate it. Fear has its use 'as a monitor to quicken our industry and keep us on our guard against the approaches of evil'. (*115*) Fear should be overcome, not by pride, vainglory or rage, but by reason and courage. 'Fortitude is the guard and support of the other virtues.' (*115*) 'True fortitude I take to be the quiet possession of a man's self and an undisturbed doing his duty, whatever evil besets or danger lies in his way.' Children should be kept from frights when young. 'Let not fearful apprehensions be talked into them nor terrible objects surprise them.' (*115*) Servants are likely to use bugbear thoughts and fear of the dark to secure obedience. 'If children were let alone, they would be no more afraid in the dark than in broad sunshine; they would in their turns as much welcome the one for sleep as the other to play in.' (*138*) Locke is modern in regarding fear of the dark as something induced rather than as something natural. Children should 'by gentle degrees' be accustomed to things they are afraid of. Locke gives a good description of gradually accustoming a child to a frog.

Cruelty. 'One thing I have frequently observed in children, that when they have got possession of any poor creature, they are apt to use it ill; they often torment and treat very roughly young birds, butterflies and such other poor animals which fall into their hands, and that with a seeming kind of pleasure.' (*116*) Possibly Locke underestimates the strength of genuine curiosity. But he advises that children should be encouraged to keep pets, provided they personally look after them. This is very wise advice. Many a modern parent has found herself badly stuck with a puppy, hamster, or collection of slow-worms, when her offspring has either lost interest or gone back to school or to stay with friends. On the subject of *forwardness*, Locke advises the encouragement of inquisitiveness, but not of pertness. (*122*) He calls *idleness* 'this sauntering humour', which is 'one of the hardest to be cured where it is natural'. (*123*) The parent should carefully observe, to see whether the idleness is about a specific task (e.g. 'his book') or a general temper. If the former, reason with him, shame him by laughing, or in the last resort make him spend all his time in the play that he prefers to his book, until he is surfeited. If idleness is a general temper, try to find something the child delights in. 'Where there is no desire, there will be no industry.' (*126*) This last remark shows that Locke was alive to a very important truth of education, and should be related to the earlier discussion of his views on self-discipline. In spite of what he says in this present connexion, it is doubtful whether Locke fully appreciated the importance of an overall sense of purpose in a deeper and more enduring sense. If necessary, Locke goes on, set the child a regular bodily labour, to get him a habit of doing something. There is clearly a certain contradiction between these two last prescriptions. If Locke recognized that there could be no effort without interest, it is difficult to believe that he really thought that a child would come to like a task by repeated practice; he does not seem to have reckoned with contra-suggestibility. Finally, *dis-*

honesty. Lying should 'be always . . . spoke of before him with the utmost detestation as a quality so wholly inconsistent with the name and character of a gentleman that nobody of any credit can bear the imputation of a lie'. *(131)* If rebuke does not check lying, 'you must come to blows'. *(131)* Locke may have recalled Montaigne's opinion that lying 'is a hateful and accursed vice', and often neglected by parents who correct much less important faults.

4. INTELLECT

Locke's belief that reason should, and can, govern behaviour has already been illustrated. Reasoning should be encouraged in children, but within their capacity. Reasoning with children is 'the true way of dealing with them'. *(81)* 'They understand it as early as they do language; and, if I misobserve not, they love to be treated as rational creatures sooner than is imagined.' *(81)* As was noted elsewhere, Locke is modern in believing that quite young children are able to reason and understand reason provided the things they are asked to reason about are within their range of experience. 'But when I talk of reasoning, I do not intend any other but such as is suited to the child's capacity and apprehension. Nobody can think a boy of three or seven years old should be argued with as a grown man. When I say, therefore, that they must be treated as rational creatures, I mean that you should make them sensible by the mildness of your carriage and the composure even in your correction of them that what you do is reasonable in you and useful and necessary for them.' *(81)* Children are not capable of 'reasonings from remote principles. They cannot conceive the force of long deductions. The reasons that move them must be obvious, and level to their thoughts, and such as may (if I may so say) be felt and touched.' *(81)*

Locke clearly appreciates the value of curiosity and interest. 'Curiosity in children is but an appetite after knowledge and therefore ought to be encouraged in them. Mark what 'tis his mind aims at in the question and not what words he expresses it in.' *(118)* This is good practical advice for any teacher. When communication between people breaks down, it is more often than not because the same words mean one thing to one person and something else to the other. This kind of misunderstanding between teacher and pupil – on whichever side it may be – is one of the commonest causes of failure in teaching. Natural curiosity shows itself in play. Therefore 'it must be permitted children not only to divert themselves, but to do it after their own fashion, provided it be innocently and without prejudice to their health'. (108) But it is clear from other remarks that Locke thought recreation should be fairly closely supervised and controlled.

'The right way to teach children is to give them a liking and inclination to what you propose to them to be learned.' (72) Learning should not be allowed to become burdensome. 'The favourable seasons of aptitude and inclination (should) be heedfully laid hold of . . . For a child will learn three times as much when he is in tune as he will with double the time and pains when he goes awkwardly or is dragged unwillingly to it.' (74) Locke is very sound in appreciating the superiority of positive motive over negative motive; a child will learn better if he sees some purpose in learning than he will if only seeking to avoid the penalties of not learning. Children should be eased through difficulties. 'In most cases where they stick, they are not to be farther puzzled by putting them upon finding it out themselves.' (167) Yet 'I will not deny but this method may sometimes be varied and difficulties proposed on purpose to excite industry and accustom the mind to employ its own strength and sagacity in reasoning'. (167)

Locke has little use for rote-learning, which was prevalent in his day. He objects to the practice of forcing children 'to learn by heart great parcels of the authors which are taught them'. (175) 'Languages are to be learned only by reading and talking, and not by scraps of authors got by heart.' (175) Further reference is made later to Locke's views on the training of memory, in connexion with the doctrine of 'transfer of training'. On this problem Locke was a good deal sounder than much of the educational thinking of more recent times.

Although Locke was against rote-learning, and realized that discovery and experience are far more valuable than information and precept, it is clear that he would never have carried the discovery method to excess. It was in 1884 that Professor Armstrong propounded the heuristic (discovery) method of learning as a corrective to the prevailing verbalism by which, for example, elementary schoolchildren (alleged to be learning physiology) were made to repeat in chorus the Latin names of the bones in the hand. The heuristic method, as formulated, had its limitations; and, as practised, was at times carried to ridiculous excess by literal-minded disciples. That such a protest against rote-learning should still be necessary two centuries after Locke is a sad reminder of the fact that it is extremely difficult to change anything in education. History provides only too much evidence of what Professor C. H. Dobinson has called 'the retrospective fixation of education'. Whatever may have been John Locke's limitations as a prophet of educational reform, he was certainly not retrospectively fixated.

5. GENERAL METHOD

Locke prescribes a combination of firmness (especially in the early years) with kindness. Reference has already been made to his insistence on discipline. As to kindness, 'The great skill of a teacher is to get and keep the attention of his scholar'. (*167*) Therefore the teacher should 'endeavour to make what he proposes as grateful and agreeable as possible . . . Let the awe he has got upon their minds be so tempered with the constant marks of tenderness and good will . . .' (*167*) 'For all their innocent folly, playing and childish actions are to be left perfectly free and unrestrained, as far as they can consist with the respect due to those that are present.' (*63*) '. . . the chief art is to make all that they have to do sport and play too.' (*63*) 'They must not be hindered from being children or from playing or doing as children, but from doing ill; all other liberty is to be allowed them.' (*69*) As children grow older, they should be given more responsibility. 'They should be accustomed betimes to consult and make use of their reason before they give allowance to their inclinations.' (*107*) '. . . as they come to grow up in age and discretion, they may be allowed greater liberty when reason comes to speak in 'em and not passion.' (*108*)

On the problem of balancing freedom and authority, Locke says: 'To avoid the danger that is on either hand is the great art; and he that has found a way how to keep up a child's spirit easy, active and free, and yet at the same time to restrain him from many things he has a mind to and to draw him to things that are uneasy to him; he, I say, that knows how to reconcile these seeming contradictions, has, in my opinion, got the true secret of education.' (*46*)

Example and practice are better than precept. Practice begets habits which 'operate of themselves'. (*66*) 'Make but few laws, but see they be well observed when once made.' (*65*) The teacher should always be honest. 'As children's enquiries are not to be slighted, so also great care is to be taken that they never receive deceitful and eluding answers. They easily perceive when they are slighted or deceived.' (*120*) Teaching should be methodically planned. Begin with 'that which is plain and simple' (*180*), and then add step by step. 'And when anyone has learned anything himself, there is no such way to fix it in his memory and to encourage him to go on as to set him to teach it to others.' (*180*)

Locke's remarks in the last paragraph are excellent examples of his accurate observation and shrewd wisdom. In his memorable summary of the 'secret of education', in the paragraph before, he goes to the root of a problem which every teacher must encounter, but which has no cut-and-dried solution.

6. INCENTIVES

Work in general should be enjoyable; and motives should be intrinsic rather than extraneous. Locke is doubtful of the value of punishments and rewards, though they cannot be altogether avoided. 'I am very apt to think that great severity of punishment does but very little good, nay, great harm in education; and I believe it will be found that, *ceteris paribus*, those children who have been most chastised seldom make the best men.' (*43*) 'Whatsoever rigour is necessary, it is more to be used the younger children are.' (*43*)

On corporal punishment Locke says: 'The usual lazy and short way by chastisement and the rod, which is the only instrument of government that tutors generally know or ever think of, is the most unfit of any to be used in education, because it tends to both those mischiefs which . . . are the Scylla and Charybdis which on the one hand or the other ruin all that miscarry.' (*47*) On the one hand, it does not contribute to the mastery of our natural propensity to indulge physical pleasure and avoid physical pain, but encourages it. On the other hand, it will make the child hate the things with which it is associated. 'Such a sort of slavish discipline makes a slavish temper.' (*50*) Passionate chiding should be avoided as should blows. Words should be 'grave, kind and sober'. (*77*) Locke, however, recommends beating for 'obstinacy or rebellion'; adding that 'the shame of the whipping and not the pain should be the greatest part of the punishment'. (*78*) '. . . stubbornness and an obstinate disobedience' must be mastered with blows; 'for there is no other remedy'. (*78*) He refers to the case of a 'prudent and kind mother' who whipped her little daughter eight times on the same morning before she could obtain a compliance. (*78*) Beating should not be done at once, 'lest passion mingle with it'. (*83*) We may contrast the famous remark of Sanderson of Oundle: 'Never punish except in anger.' The story is told that Sanderson's printer inadvertently provoked a spontaneous eruption of wrath by putting a query against the word 'except' in the galley proof! Locke advises that corporal punishment should be administered by a servant in the parent's presence, so that the parent's authority shall be demonstrated, but 'the child's aversion for the pain it suffers rather to be turned on the person that immediately inflicts'. (*83*) One cannot but think Locke's logic is too fine-spun in this connexion, and that the subtle distinction would hardly signify to the ordinary juvenile victim. But the idea of employing a subordinate to perform the rites is interesting, in view of the contemporary practice in the schools of employing ushers 'under the headmaster, equal with the chief scholars', and, into modern times, prefects, to deal with routine disciplinary business.

Locke, in general, condemns the use of rewards as irrelevant. He would not have approved of bicycles and transistors as a stimulus to

8 · The Care of the Child

Locke's remarks about bodily health occupy about one-tenth of his whole book on Education. It must be remembered that Locke was himself a qualified physician. Though some of his opinions seem strange to the modern reader, his views were on the whole sensible, though fairly austere; his puritan tradition comes out clearly in his attitude towards the body.

As a doctor, Locke naturally holds that there can be no *mens sana* unless *in corpore sano*. The opening sentence of the book is: 'A sound Mind in **a** sound body is a short but full description of a happy state in this world.' (*1*) He sums up his views in these words: 'And thus I have done with what concerns the body and health, which reduces itself to these few and easily observable rules. Plenty of open air, exercise and sleep; plain diet, no wine or strong drink, and very little or no physic; not too warm and strait clothing; especially the head and feet kept cold, and the feet often used to cold water, and exposed to wet.' (*30*) 'Gentlemen should use their children as the honest farmers and substantial yeomen do theirs.' (*4*) And he alludes disapprovingly to 'fond mothers and foolish servants'. (*13*) Most of Locke's prescriptions would have had the strong support of Lord Baden Powell, the founder of the Scout movement.

Food should be plain. 'I should think a good piece of well-made and well-baked brown bread, sometimes with and sometimes without butter or cheese, would be often the best breakfast for my young master.' (*14*) Breakfast cereals had not been invented in Locke's day! 'His drink should be only small beer.' (*16*) Children should not

G

be allowed to drink whenever they like, lest custom makes them thirsty every hour. (*18*) Locke refers to a baby who 'though he could not speak, yet he drank more in twenty-four hours than I did.' (*18*)

Beds should not be too comfortable. Locke stresses the importance of being able to sleep anywhere. 'The great cordial of nature is sleep.' (*22*) 'He is very unfortunate who can take his cordial only in his mother's fine gilt cup and not in a wooden dish.' (*22*) As to the amount of sleep, young children should be 'permitted to have their full satisfaction, nothing contributing more to the growth and health of children than sleep'. (*21*) They should go early to bed and rise early, 'whereby they will be accustomed to avoid the unhealthy and unsafe hours of debauchery'. (*21*). As they get older children should not be allowed excessive sleep; between the ages of seven and fourteen, sleep should be reduced by degrees to eight hours, 'which is generally rest enough for healthy grown people'. (*21*) Children should not be woken suddenly or by the shock of sudden, violent noise. (*21*) (Boarding-schools please note!)

Among forms of physical exercise, Locke advocates swimming, quoting the Roman opinion that swimming was as important as literacy.

Locke takes great interest in regular bowel actions, warning against the dangers of constipation, but urging the importance of relying on regular habit rather than on physic. One should 'solicit nature'. (*23–28*) Locke had studied this matter carefully; and his views would have been endorsed by the medical profession up to about twenty-five years ago. In quite recent times doctors have for some reason lost interest in this bodily function, and no longer greet the patient with what used to be the inevitable first inquiry.

Locke's views on health include some oddities. He is, for example, against regular hours for meals; 'for when custom has fixed his eating to certain stated periods, his stomach will expect victuals at the usual hour and grow peevish if he passes it'. (*15*) He under-estimates the importance of sugar. 'Sweetmeats of all kinds are to be avoided.' (*20*) He would not have approved of sweet rations during the war. One of his strangest notions concerns the hardening effect of exposing the feet to wet. Although in our day, protection of the feet is perhaps not considered as important as it was a generation or two ago, we should agree that Locke goes a bit far in recommending shoes that leak. Again, Locke has some curious notions about fruit; he allows strawberries, cherries, gooseberries, currants, apples, and pears (*20*), but condemns melons, peaches, and plums. (*20*) It is very notable that Locke has nothing to say about sex education.

On the whole, however, Locke's views on health are remarkably sound. His puritan bias is clear; but so also is his belief in the curative powers of nature – a belief shared by his friend Sydenham, but not at all fashionable in Locke's own time. The following passage is interesting, both for its modern ring, and also because Locke evidently did not expect his contemporaries to pay attention to what he said. 'Another thing that is of great advantage to everyone's health, but especially children's, is to be much in the open air, and as little as may be by the fire, even in winter. By this he will accustom himself also to heat and cold, shine and rain; all which, if a man's body will not endure, it will serve him to very little purpose in this world; and when he is grown up, it is too late to begin to use him to it . . . Thus the body may be brought to bear almost anything. If I should advise him to play in the wind and the sun without a hat, I doubt whether it could be borne. There would a thousand objections be made against it, which at last would amount to no more, in truth, than being sunburnt.' (*9*) Locke even recommended that girls should be exposed to the air. The elderly among us will remember that, at least up to the first decade of the present century, children always wore hats, especially in the sun.

2. THE CHILD IN THE HOME (PARENTS AND CHILDREN)

Locke is fully alive to the importance of impressions made in the early years of life. The foundations of right values should be laid in infancy. 'Those therefore that intend ever to govern their children should begin it whilst they are very little, and look that they perfectly comply with the will of their parents.' (*40*) He deplores the bad habits (of violence, vanity, intemperance, gluttony) that were

prevalent in society in his day, insists that the basis of good character is self-control under the guidance of reason, and vigorously
criticizes the over-indulgence of children by many parents. 'The
fondling must be taught to strike and call names, must have what he
cries for, and do what he pleases. Thus parents, by humouring and
cockering them when little, corrupt the principles of nature in their
children, and wonder afterwards to taste the bitter waters, when
they have themselves poisoned the fountain. For when their children
are grown up, and these ill habits with them; when they are now too
big to be dandled and their parents can no longer make use of them
as playthings, then they complain that the brats are untoward and
perverse; then they are offended to see them wilful and are troubled
with those ill humours which they themselves infused and fomented
in them; and then, perhaps too late, would be glad to get out those
weeds which their own hands have planted, and which now have
taken too deep root to be easily extirpated.' (*35*) 'For if the child
must have grapes or sugar-plums when he has a mind to them, rather
than make the poor baby cry, or be out of humour; why, when he
is grown up, must he not be satisfied too, if his desires carry him to
wine or women?' (*36*)

Parents should make sure of their authority. They should be
'absolute governors'. 'Would you have your son obedient to you
when past a child, be sure then to establish the authority of a father
as soon as he is capable of submission and can understand in whose
power he is. If you would have him stand in awe of you, imprint
it in his infancy; and as he approaches more to a man, admit him
nearer to your familiarity.' (*40*) 'I imagine everyone will judge it
reasonable that their children, when little, should look upon their
parents as their lords, their absolute governors, and as such stand in
awe of them; and when they come to riper years, they should look
on them as their best, as their only sure friends, and as such love and
reverence them.' (*41*) 'Fear and awe ought to give you the first
power over their minds, and love and friendship in later years to
hold it.' (*42*) Locke quotes Juvenal: 'Maxima debetur pueris
reverentia.' (*71*)

If Locke's injunctions to parents appear harsh, we must remember that he found far too much over-indulgence among the upper classes of his day. We must also, in fairness to Locke, remember that, as was shown in passages quoted in an earlier chapter, he believed that firmness should be tempered with kindness, that the treatment meted out to the child ought always, so far as possible, be shown to be reasonable, and appreciated by the child as reasonable, and also that liberty and play are needed by the child in the process of growing. It must not be forgotten that Locke was no advocate of corporal punishment. Children, in short, are to be treated 'tenderly', though telling lies is regarded as a fault to be treated with special severity. (99)

At the same time it must be recognized that, although he believed that children have rights, which should be respected, he also believed that adults have rights which children ought to respect. One of his reasons for objecting to children's crying is that the noise is a nuisance to other people. Since Locke's day, libertarian views on education have at times swung so far in the child's direction as to suggest that, in education, everything should be sacrificed to the 'natural' development of the child. Apart from the fact that human society is not 'natural' anyway, is it reactionary to suggest that one thing children have to learn is not to annoy other people, including their elders?

Where Locke's views are, perhaps, open to criticism is in his failure to allow sufficiently for contra-suggestibility. The same point has been noticed elsewhere, in a discussion of Locke's views of habit-formation; he too readily assumes that oft-repeated actions will 'stick'. What Locke never makes really clear (though he certainly implies it) is that the most important thing in a young child's life is love. Provided the child feels loved, considerable firmness can be used without ill effect; in fact, the child needs a strong supporting framework of imposed discipline before he can grow into the maturer stage of self-discipline.

The other side of the coin is that, where love is both given and received sincerely, 'spoiling', in the ordinary sense of indulgence, does considerably less permanent harm than used to be thought. Either way, the most important thing is that the child should feel loved, and should *trust* those who look after him. Otherwise, he will tell lies from fear, and will develop all kinds of pathological symptoms (such as pilfering) to supply in fantasy what he knows he lacks in reality.

Locke is very sensible on the subject of toys, recommending that simple playthings made by the children themselves are better than expensive bought toys. Of playthings he says: 'Though it be agreed they should have of several sorts, yet I think they should have none bought for them. . . . A smooth pebble, a piece of paper, the mother's bunch of keys or anything they cannot hurt themselves with serves as much to divert little children as those more chargeable and curious toys from the shops, which are presently put out of order and broken.' (*130*) Toys which they cannot make (such as tops, battledores) may be bought; these they need for exercise.

It was remarked in an earlier chapter that Locke's views on the proper relation between father and son were closely based on his own relations with his father, to whom he was very loyal. As the boy grows older, authority should change to friendship. 'The sooner you treat him as a man, the sooner he will begin to be one; and if you admit him into serious discourses sometimes with you, you will insensibly raise his mind.' (*95*) He recommends fathers to take their sons into confidence about matters of business – 'their estates and concerns'. (*96*) Sons should be encouraged to take part in conversation. 'Particularly in morality, prudence and breeding, cases should be put to him, and his opinion asked. This way lets things into the mind . . . whereas words at best are faint representations.' (*98*) But, as always, Locke does not expect too much. 'You must not expect his inclination should be just as yours nor that at twenty he should have the same thoughts you have at fifty.' (*97*) There is, however, value in mutual confidence. 'Would your son engage in some frolic or take a vagary, were it not much better he should do it with than without your knowledge?' (*96*)

Finally, Locke would have the support of all, in any age, who know anything about education in his insistence that actions speak louder than words, and practice is more effective than precept. 'You must do nothing before him which you would not have him imitate.' (*71*) An easier maxim to state than to act upon; but a salutary reminder of the educator's personal responsibility.

3. SCHOOL OR TUTOR

Locke's poor view of schools has already been noted. 'School-masters cannot be expected to have fifty or a hundred scholars under his eye any longer than they are in school together; nor can it be expected that he should instruct them successfully in anything but their books.' (*70*) He advises parents not to 'hazard your son's innocence and virtue for a little Greek and Latin'. (*70*) 'Virtue is harder to be got than a knowledge of the world.' (*70*) 'Courage and steadiness . . . lie not in roughness and ill breeding.' (*70*) 'It is not the waggeries or cheats practised amongst schoolboys, it is not their roughness to one another, or their well-laid plots of robbing an orchard together, that make an able man; but the principles of justice, generosity, and sobriety, joined with observation and industry, qualities which I judge schoolboys do not learn much of one another.' (*70*) 'Vice, if we may believe the general complaint, ripens so fast nowadays and runs up to seed so early in young people, that it is impossible to keep a lad from the spreading contagion if you will venture him abroad in the herd and trust to chance or his own inclination for the choice of his company at school.' (*70*)

It is clear that Locke has more in mind than merely the inherent defects of schools as such. He is disturbed by the general decline of standards in his time. One can speculate on what he might have said about teenage rowdyism and sexual precocity in our own day. 'By what fate vice hath so thriven amongst us these years past, and by what hands it has been nursed up into so uncontrolled a dominion, I shall leave to others to enquire. I wish that those who complain of the great decay of Christian piety and virtue everywhere, and of learning and of acquired improvements in the gentry of this generation, would consider how to retrieve them in the next.' (*70*)

Locke advises parents to engage a tutor rather than send their sons to school. Although he quite fairly admits the fact that good tutors are hard to come by, we have to remember that he is nevertheless comparing good tutors with bad schools.

As for the qualities of a good tutor, character is more important than scholarship. The tutor 'should himself be well-bred'. (*93*) 'The tailor may make his clothes modish and the dancing master give fashion to his motions; yet none of these, though they set off well, make a well-bred gentleman . . . Breeding alone is that which sets a gloss upon all his other good qualities.' (*93*) The tutor's example is paramount. 'It will be to no purpose for his tutor to talk of the restraint of the passions whilst any of his own are let loose.' (*89*) The boy's father should treat the tutor with respect if the boy is to do the same (*88*); the tutor should be kept away from the servants, who are the most dangerous source of bad examples. (*89*)

'Besides being well-bred, the tutor should know the world well, the ways, the humours, the follies, the cheats, the faults of the age . . . and particularly of the country he lives in.' (*94*) 'He should acquaint him with the true state of the world and dispose him to think no man better or worse, wiser or foolisher than he really is. Thus, by safe and insensible degrees he will pass from a boy to a man, which is the most hazardous step in the whole course of life.' (*94*) 'The only fence against the world is a thorough knowledge of it.' (*94*) Fathers should not forget 'of how much more use it is to judge right of men and manage his affairs wisely with them than to speak Greek or Latin or argue in mood or figure or to have his head filled with the abstruse speculations of natural philosophy and meta-physics'. (*94*) 'The great work of a governor is to fashion the carriage and form the mind; to settle in his pupil good habits and the principles of virtue and wisdom; to give him by little and little a view of mankind, and work him into a love and imitation of what is excellent and praiseworthy; and, in the prosecution of it, to give him vigour, activity and industry.' (*94*)

Good tutors, as Locke recognized, are difficult to get. 'Spare no care nor cost' (*92*), he says. A good tutor will not be obtained for 'ordinary salaries'. (*90*) This advice of Locke's must be read against the background of conditions at that time, when tutors were so poorly paid that a good footman might earn more. In a letter to Locke, Mr Molyneux was evidently prepared to go to some lengths: 'He should eat at my own table, and have his lodging, washing, firing, and candlelight in my house, in a good handsome apartment; and besides this I should allow him 20*l* per annum.'

No wise father would dispute the importance of securing the best possible tutor for his son. ' 'Tis not good husbandry to make his fortune rich and his mind poor.' (*90*) Nor would a wise father dispute Locke's view that character is more important in the tutor than scholarship; books can carry the boy farther in scholarship but not in character. Indeed, the point has been already conceded by the fact of settling for a tutor rather than for a school, since no tutor can be expected to be a specialist in all subjects (it is clear on which side Locke would have been in the modern argument about form-masters *versus* specialist teachers). At the same time it must be admitted that Locke's whole discussion of tutors and their qualities is somewhat unreal, since we never discover where the ideal tutor is to be found. In fact, we are left with the suspicion that this rare bird does not exist. At the same time there is plenty of evidence to corroborate Locke's low opinion of schools at that time. The achievement of education in the seventeenth century had its difficulties.

One thing that does emerge clearly from Locke's remarks about tutors – and which has relevance to us notwithstanding all the differences between his world and ours – is his firm belief that teaching is essentially a person-to-person relation – a partnership in the pursuit of truth. There should be understanding and trust between teacher and pupil. 'Familiarity of discourse, if it can become a father to his son, may much more be condescended to by a tutor to his pupil.' (*98*)

9 · Programme of Studies

Locke's choice of subjects to be studied is pragmatic. The test is usability. His practical approach saves him from erroneous doctrines of 'formal training' or 'training the mind'. What he says about memorization is very modern. Of the current belief that learning by heart improves memory, he says: 'I could wish this were said with as much authority of reason as it is with forwardness of assurance, and that this practice were established upon good observation more than old custom; for it is evident that strength of memory is owing to a happy constitution and not to any habitual improvement got by exercise.' (176) He anticipates the modern answer to the problem of 'transfer of training' by two hundred and fifty years. 'What the mind is intent upon and careful of, that it remembers best'. (176)

What is remarkable about Locke's model curriculum is not that it is different from today's, which it inevitably is, but that it is not much *more* different. Except for English literature (of which, in his day, there was less than there is now), the basic subjects of the modern curriculum are there – the three Rs, English composition, history, geography, languages, and the sciences. Manual crafts, physical activities, leisure interests, are there too; though his exclusion of poetry and music is remarkable. Broadly speaking, the schools of this country had to wait a good many generations before a curriculum as broad and liberal as Locke's became general. Those who know something of the history of education in England will not need to be reminded how resistant the grammar school tradition was to the liberal example of the dissenting academies in the seventeenth and eighteenth centuries. Legislation against the nonconformists after the Restoration of 1660 drove the dissenters out of the established schools and universities. They began to establish their own. In the first half of the eighteenth century there were over thirty of these academies, with a curriculum which included, besides Greek and Latin, some logic, mathematics, and science, together with modern subjects like history, geography, French, and Italian.

Although John Locke's allegiance to the established church was never in doubt, his educational sympathies were clearly with the dissenting academies. And it is one of the misfortunes of our educational history that these academies did not have more impact on the general pattern of education in England.

Joseph Priestley, a pioneer of science teaching, taught for some years at Warrington Academy (he also lectured on languages, history, and geography). In his *Essay on a Course of Liberal Education for Civil and Active Life*, Priestley said: 'Formerly none but the clergy were thought to have any occasion for learning. It was natural therefore that the whole plan of education, from the grammar school to the finishing at the university, should be calculated for their use.' But, by his time, 'a different and better furniture of mind is requisite to be brought into the business of life'. Locke, writing nearly a century earlier, was fully in accord with this point of view.

Here follow Locke's main observations on the subjects of the curriculum.

READING

Locke would begin the learning of reading very young. 'When he can talk, 'tis time he should begin to learn to read . . . Great care is to be taken that it be never made as a business to him, nor he look on it as a task . . . I have always had a fancy that learning might be made a play and recreation to children . . . There may be dice and playthings with the letters on them to teach children the alphabet by playing.' (*148*) Quintilian, and Plato before him, had recommended that lessons should take the form of play. 'I know a person of great quality, more yet to be honoured for his learning and virtue than for his rank and high place, who by pasting on the six vowels (for in our language Y is one) on the six sides of a die and the remaining consonants on the sides of three other dice has made this a play for his children, that he shall win who at one cast throws most words on these four dice.' (*151*)

Modern opinion does not support Locke's insistence on the early learning of reading. In fact, there is evidence that time apparently lost by the postponement of any kind of formal learning can be quickly made up.

As to suitable reading matter, Locke was limited by the scarcity of literature suitable for children in his day. It is only in quite modern times that books for children have been written in any quantity. He condemns 'useless trumpery', and recommends *Aesop's Fables*, 'which, being stories apt to delight and entertain a child, may yet afford useful reflections to a grown man'. (*156*) He also recommends *Reynard the Fox*, a famous 'beast-epic' of Germany, a satire on German Society in feudal times. Reynard the Fox is the Church, always trying to get the better of Isengrin the Wolf, the feudal baron. It was published in 1498; but Caxton had published it in English in 1481.

Locke has views on the reading of the Bible which would appeal to the *avant-garde* of research in religious education today. 'As for the Bible . . . I think the promiscuous reading of it through by chapters as they lie in order is so far from being of any advantage to children, either for the perfecting their reading or principling their religion, that perhaps a worse could not be found.' (*158*) He recommends the stories of Joseph and his brethren, David and Jonathan, David and Goliath. It is notable, and perhaps surprising, that he does not recommend any New Testament stories.

WRITING

'When he can read English well, it will be seasonable to enter him in writing; and here the first thing should be taught him is to hold his pen right.' (*160*) 'When he can write well and quick, I think it may be convenient, not only to continue the exercise of his hand in writing, but also to improve the use of it farther in drawing – a thing very useful to a gentleman in several occasions, but especially if he travel, as that which helps a man often to express in a few lines well put together what a whole sheet of paper in writing would not be able to represent and make intelligible.' (*161*) These last remarks of Locke's are very much to the point. Until the invention of photography rather more than a hundred years ago, travels in foreign countries were often enriched by pictorial record.

Modern practice in the teaching of writing obviously differs from Locke's prescriptions. We teach reading and writing side by side; and we would encourage drawing and painting before rather than after the child has learnt to write.

ENGLISH COMPOSITION

Locke is very much alive to the practical value of skill in the use of the English language. 'To write and speak correctly gives a grace and gains a favourable attention to what one has to say; and since it is English that an English gentleman will have constant use of, that is the language he should chiefly cultivate, and wherein most care should be taken to polish and perfect his style.' (*189*) 'There can scarce be a greater defect in a gentleman than not to express himself well either in writing or speaking . . . it might not be amiss to make children, as soon as they are capable of it, often to tell a story of anything they know . . . When they can tell tales pretty well, then it may be the time to make them write them.' (*189*) Locke is in line with modern practice in regarding spoken composition as the preliminary to written composition. We should also agree that children should be 'taught to express their own plain, easy sense without any incoherence, confusion or roughness'. (*189*)

In condemning the exercise of writing Latin verses, Locke objects to writing poetry of any kind. Locke clearly had a 'thing' about poetry. 'If he have a poetic vein, it is to me the strangest thing in the world that the father should desire or suffer it to be cherished or improved . . . I know not what reason a father can have to wish his son a poet, who does not desire to have him bid defiance to all other callings and business.' (*174*) Of Parnassus he says: 'It is a pleasant air, but a barren soil; and there are very few instances of those who have added to their patrimony by anything they have reaped from thence.' One can understand a father's anxiety if his son proposed to make his living by writing poetry; but Locke seems to rule it out even as an elegant accomplishment. Poetry and gaming, he observes, 'usually go together'.

LANGUAGES

In Locke's time there was great over-emphasis on Latin. Locke seeks to diminish this emphasis. And he advises teaching, not by grammar rules, but by oral methods or the use of interlinear translations. Latin he regarded as necessary for a gentleman; Greek, though valuable, was not necessary. French should be taught orally, and begun before Latin. Locke would no doubt have approved of French in the primary school. 'As soon as he can speak English, 'tis time for him to learn some other language. This nobody doubts of when French is proposed; and the reason is because people are accustomed to the right way of teaching that language, which is by talking it into children in constant conversation, and not by grammatical rules. The Latin tongue would easily be taught the same way if his tutor, being constantly with him, would talk nothing else to him and make him answer still in the same language.' (*162*) 'When he can speak and read French well, which in this method is usually in a year or two, he should proceed to Latin.' (*163*)

Latin is 'absolutely necessary to a gentleman'. (*164*) As to the method of teaching Latin, '. . . if you will consider it, Latin is no more unknown to a child when he comes into the world than English; and yet he learns English without master, rule or grammar; and so might he Latin too, as Tully did, if he had somebody always to talk to him in this language'. (*165*) If you cannot get a tutor who can teach Latin orally (the difficulty of teaching orally was the great obstacle to the spread, in our time, of the Perse School's Direct Method), Locke recommends, as the next best thing, 'taking some easy and pleasant book, such as *Aesop's Fables*, and writing the English translation (made as literal as it can be) in one line, and the

Latin words which answer each of them just over it in another'. (*167*) This method was known in Anglo-Saxon times.

'For the exercise of his writing let him sometimes translate Latin into English.' (*169*) Locke has no use for 'themes' or verses. Themes were Latin orations on some Latin saying such as 'Non licet in bello bis peccare' (one cannot afford to make the same mistake twice in war). Such exercises were very artificial and mostly on topics remote from the pupil's experience. Locke's objection to them was sound, and was supported nearly two centuries later by John Stuart Mill. Locke's comment on Greek is: 'I . . . will add that no man can pass for a scholar that is ignorant of the Greek tongue. But I am not here considering the education of a professed scholar, but of a gentleman.' (*195*)

GRAMMAR

Locke condemns the mass of rules for accidence and syntax used in his time. He realized that the detailed study of grammar should come only after a working knowledge of the language has been acquired. And he urges the importance of knowing the grammar of one's own language. It is worth noting that J. S. Mill regarded grammar as the beginning of the analysis of the thinking process.

'. . . grammar has its place too. But this I think I may say, there is a great deal more stir made with it than there needs and those tormented about it to whom it does not at all belong; I mean children at the age wherein they are usually perplexed with it in grammar schools.' (*168*) '. . . there are ladies who, without knowing what tenses and participles, adverbs and prepositions are, speak as properly and correctly (they might take it for an ill compliment if I said as any country schoolmaster) as most gentlemen who have been bred up in the ordinary methods of grammar schools.' (*168*) The serious scholar needs the detailed study of grammar; but the time for it is when a working command of the language has already been gained. It is a pity that the schools took so long to listen to what Locke had to say about grammar.

SCIENCE

We must remember that, in Locke's time, none of the sciences as we know them, except possibly astronomy, was sufficiently matured and defined for school teaching. To Locke Science meant what we would call the physical sciences plus metaphysics, or what in his day was called Natural Philosophy. (The survival, in our universities, of the degree of Ph.D. is a reminder of this wider meaning of philosophy.)

It is interesting to note that, notwithstanding Locke's great emphasis on the empirical approach to truth, and his demand that belief should be based on evidence, he also held that there are limits to the reach of human reason, and consequently an element of mystery in all truth. In this recognition of mystery Locke is more in tune with the great modern scientists than with the materialists of a century ago. It was Sir Lawrence Bragg, one of the most distinguished physicists of our generation, who, in a recent television interview, affirmed the place of revelation in scientific discovery ('When you discover something, it is as if you had been told something').

'The works of nature are contrived by a wisdom, and operated by ways, too far surpassing our faculties to discover or capacities to conceive for us ever to be able to reduce them into a science.' (*190*) Yet 'I would not deter anyone from the study of nature because all the knowledge we have or possibly can have of it cannot be brought into a science.' (*193*) '. . . the incomparable Mr Newton has shown how far mathematics applied to some parts of nature may, upon principles that matter of fact justify, carry us in the knowledge of some, as I may so call them, particular provinces of the incomprehensible universe . . . we might in time hope to be furnished with more and certain knowledge of certain parts of this stupendous machine than hitherto we could have expected.' (*194*)

Although his idiom is strange to us, Locke's warning against materialistic thinking is relevant. Natural Philosophy, he says, has two parts, 'one comprehending spirits . . . the other bodies. The first of these is usually referred to as metaphysics.' (*190*) The study of spirits, in his view, should come *before* the study of bodies (or, as we might say, some general philosophy before concentration on the physical sciences) 'because matter is so apt to possess the mind that it may leave no room for spirits'. (*190, 192*) He recommends that a good history of the Bible should be read by young people, and refers (*192*) to a theory of the Flood as caused by a Divine alteration of the Earth's centre of gravity for a time.

OTHER SUBJECTS

While the child is learning French and Latin, he should begin arithmetic, geography, chronology, history, and geometry. These subjects, Locke suggests, might be taught through the medium of French or Latin!

To our way of thinking, Locke's notion of *geography* is very limited, consisting of a number of facts to be learnt (what we used to know as 'capes and bays') and the methods of finding latitude and longitude. He scarcely recognizes the interplay of man and his environment.

In *geometry* Locke advises the first six books of Euclid, and a knowledge of the Copernican system of astronomy (which was not much more than one hundred and fifty years old at that time).

In *arithmetic*, Locke believes in practical application, and recommends that the boy should learn the use of maps and how to keep accounts. (*210–11*)

In Locke's day *chronology* presented problems which it does not present to us. There were various chronological systems in practical use; and the Gregorian Calendar (authorized by Papal edict in 1582 in place of the Julian) was not adopted in Britain until 1752.

Locke believed strongly in the value of studying *history*, 'which is the great mistress of prudence and civil knowledge'. (*184*) 'As nothing teaches, so nothing delights more than history.' (*184*) No history textbooks, as we understand them, existed at that time; and history was mostly read in Latin. For reasons of circumstance, therefore, Locke was unable to develop his ideas about the study of history as he might have done had greater resources been available. The critical analysis and evaluation of historical sources belongs to a

H

later age. Although separately discussed by Locke, we may take in this connexion his view that every gentleman should have some knowledge of the law, government, and constitution of his country. (*187*)

Locke distrusts the formal teaching of *logic and rhetoric*, at that time part of the traditional curriculum for older pupils, and his belief in the practical approach appears again. 'Reasoning and eloquence are not learnt by rule, but by practice and example . . . if you would have your son reason well, let him read Chillingworth' (a seventeenth-century theologian); 'and if you would have him speak well, let him be conversant in Tully' (Cicero) 'to give him the true idea of eloquence'. (*188*) Sir Winston Churchill held the same view as that given in Locke's additional precept: '. . . and let him read those things that are well writ in English, to perfect his style in the purity of our language'.

PRACTICAL ACTIVITIES

Locke did not by any means think in terms of a purely academic curriculum. Dancing is recommended as an aid to 'graceful motions' and 'manliness and a becoming confidence'. (*67, 196*) Riding is recommended; and fencing is allowed, though wrestling is preferred. (*198*) Music is dismissed: '. . . it wastes so much of a young man's time to gain but a moderate skill in it'. (*197*) Of the arts, painting is 'that which of all others would please me best', except that 'ill painting is one of the worst things in the world', and 'it is a sedentary occupation'. (*203*) Locke recommends a great variety of crafts, including carpentry, engineering, metal work, working precious stones, grinding optical glasses. (*204, 209*) Although Locke would include practical subjects in his curriculum, there is no evidence that he really appreciated what the practice of arts and crafts (even to a modest standard) can do for the personality.

One of the notable features of Locke's scheme is his belief that every gentleman's son ought to learn a trade. Even recreation should be planned with an eye to 'what will afterwards be profitable'. 'I would have him learn a trade, a manual trade, nay two or three, but one more particularly.' (*201*) 'Skill not only in languages and learned sciences, but in painting, turning, gardening, tempering and working in iron and all other useful arts is worth the having.' (*202*) Apart from the usefulness of these skills, those exercises are advocated that are 'necessary or useful for health'. (*202*) Locke had lived through times of great social disturbance, when many families had sustained serious changes of fortune. It is not surprising that he should have urged gentlemen to equip their sons to be able to fend for themselves in case of need. Nor is it surprising that, in the comparatively carefree atmosphere of Restoration England, nobody paid much attention to his counsel about learning a trade.

Life, according to Locke, must have room for leisure interests. 'Nothing can come into the account of recreation that is not done with delight.' (*197*) At the same time, 'recreation is not being idle (as everyone may observe) but easing the wearied part by change of business'. (*206*) He advises against learning cards and dice so that the young man may be 'incapacitated for those dangerous temptations and encroaching wastes of useful time'. (*208*) Many people of our own generation have found it prudent not to learn how to play bridge; so that one could say: 'I don't play', and so avoid constant pressure to spend hour after yawning hour at the card-table.

A most valuable recreation, in Locke's view, is foreign travel. But he thought travel was undertaken at the wrong age. Young gentlemen return little improved by their travel, which could be more profitably undertaken in childhood (to learn languages) or in early manhood (to extend experience). The usual age for travel in Locke's time was sixteen to twenty-one. Locke advises travel at seven to fourteen, or, with a tutor, after twenty-one. Travel has great advantages, not only for the learning of languages but for 'improvement in wisdom and prudence by seeing men and conversing with people of tempers, customs and ways of living different from one another and especially from those of his parish and neighbourhood'. (*212*) Locke is ironical about the prevailing custom. 'The young lad must not be ventured abroad at eight or ten for fear of what may happen to the tender child, though he then runs ten times less risk than at sixteen or eighteen. Nor must he stay at home till that dangerous, heady age be over, because he must be back again by one and twenty to marry and propagate.' (*216*) Locke does not recognize any need to prepare for marriage. He lightly dismisses the matter with: '. . . the young gentleman being got within view of matrimony, 'tis time to leave him to his mistress'. (*216*)

RELIGION

Locke has very little to say about religious education; and what he does say is ethical and pragmatic. 'There ought very early to be imprinted on his mind a true notion of God, as of the independent Supreme Being, Author and Maker of all things, from Whom we receive all our good, Who loves us and gives us all things.' (*136*) He bases morality on our duty to God, and recommends morning and evening prayers. Strangely, he makes no reference to Christ – though he has something to say about goblins! He holds that the Lord's Prayer, the Creeds, and the Ten Commandments should be learnt by heart. We have already noticed his reservations about the reading of the Bible by young children, though he thinks a grasp of Bible history is valuable at a later age, and such selections from the Bible as will give children 'a notion and belief of spirits'. (*190*)

In general, Locke's views on education must be regarded as the amateur, slightly garrulous reflections of an elderly bachelor. But what he says is full of common sense, often wittily and astringently expressed, and represents an enormous advance on educational practice in his own time. He was fifty-two when he wrote the letters to Edward Clarke, and sixty-one when the book was published in 1693.

Locke gives little indication of the ages at which the various stages of development are reached. Nor is there much indication of methodology. It must be remembered that, though some educational writers of those days had more practical teaching experience than Locke, there was no scientific study of children or of education as we understand it.

Finally, Locke is very modest about his book. 'I would not have it thought that I look on it as a just treatise on this subject. There are a thousand other things that may need consideration.' (*216*) In the three centuries since Locke's book on education appeared, we have been studying and arguing about some of the 'thousand other things'. But it is doubtful whether his basic principles have been improved upon, or his native wisdom exceeded.

Notes

CHAPTER 3

1 *Westminster School*, Rupert Hart-Davis, 1965, p. 9.
2 *Logic*, I, vi.
3 The portraits described above are in the National Portrait Gallery (the 1704 Kneller being a copy); and the information about them is taken from the *Catalogue Raisonné* of the Seventeenth-Century Portraits, by David Piper.
4 *John Locke*, 1957, p. xi.

CHAPTER 4

1 Editorial Foreword to O'Connor's *John Locke*.
2 Aaron, *John Locke*, p. 302.
3 Cranston, *John Locke*, p. 279.

CHAPTER 5

1 He retained his pre-Freudian faith in the capacity of reason to handle experience; and he tended to attribute to empirical knowledge something of the certainty pertaining to the traditional classical theory of knowledge.
2 He was thirty-five when he was entrusted with the education of Shaftesbury's son, then a boy of fifteen or sixteen. Some years later this boy's son was placed in Locke's care from the age of three to twelve, when he went to Winchester; but the boy's actual instruction was done by a governess. In 1677, when Locke was forty-five, he took direct charge of the son of Sir John Banks, a friend of Shaftesbury's, for some two years in France.
3 'As the strength of the body lies chiefly in being able to endure hardships, so also does that of the mind. . . . The first thing they should learn to know should be that they were not to have anything because it pleased them, but because it was thought fit for them.'

4 A recent television programme contained an interview with a Los Angeles father, who regarded himself as below the poverty line ($3,000–$4,000 a year), but who said that boys must be given bicycles at eleven and cars at seventeen; otherwise they would steal them and get themselves into court.

CHAPTER 6

1 Quoted from I. Parker's *Dissenting Academies in England*.

Appendix: Note on the Mellon Collection of Locke Papers

In 1960 the American, Paul Mellon, presented a collection of John Locke material to the Bodleian Library. Mr Peter Laslett published a description of this material in *The Times Literary Supplement* (11 March 1960). I have seen these papers in the Bodleian.

The Mellon gift includes eleven manuscript volumes, covering a very wide range of subjects – theology, science, medicine, economics, political theory, as well as natural history and notes on colonial administration.

The collection consists largely of Commonplace Books, kept with Locke's characteristic care. At the end of one of these is the weather diary, with hygroscope, thermometer, and barometer readings, which he kept from 1666–83 and 1691–1703. In it he describes the Fire of London of 1666, which he observed from Oxford. He also notes the sudden growth of interest in the arrival of swallows in England in spring and their departure in autumn. These, Mr Laslett suggests, may be the earliest recordings in our history.

The most striking feature of the Mellon collection, however, is Locke's herbarium, in two volumes. His interest in botany was related to his study of medicine. He gathered a specimen of every plant growing in Oxford and in the Oxford botanical garden, and dried and pressed them between sheets of his pupils' written exercises. In all he made a collection of some 3,000 plants, carefully named in Latin and English. They are most beautifully pressed and arranged; and, after three hundred years, some are still so perfect in delicate detail that they might have been picked yesterday. Though to a great extent the colours have faded, some of the colours have survived surprisingly well. Locke's collection may well be among the oldest surviving specimens of English wild flowers. The flowers themselves, and their English names, have not changed. Red campion, snowdrop, wild snapdragon and daffodil, foxglove, heartsease, yellow iris, melilot, rosebay willowherb – they are all there between the sheets of thick, hand-made paper, inscribed on one side with Latin exercises, and the plain sides used to mount the flowers.

It is a salutary experience to spend some time looking through Locke's herbarium. If he had done nothing else, he would deserve to be known to posterity for that alone. Yet his collection of flowers was one incidental activity, on the side, of this remarkable and many-sided man, who knew his way about all existing fields of thought and knowledge, and was an authority in many of them.

Also in the Mellon collection is Locke's annotated copy of the *Catalogus Horti Botanici Oxoniensis*, 1658, compiled by Philip Stephens and William Browne, in which Locke has added a number of plants not listed in the catalogue itself; there is scarcely a page that has not at least one addition in Locke's neat handwriting. The preface to the second part of the printed catalogue ends with these words, which must assuredly have appealed to Locke: 'Thus as the species of all creatures were gathered together into the Arke, comprehended as in an Epitome, so you have the plants of most parts of the world, contained in this garden where they are preserved for thy inspection, not thy plunder, and faithfully related, by the care and endeavour of   P.S.   W.B.'

Locke's own library, left at Oates, High Laver, consisted of 3,675 volumes, scrupulously arranged in numbered box-shelves, all carefully catalogued, and bearing the owner's signature. In the middle of his study was his big oak desk, made to his design, with compartments for each of his correspondents. All compromising passages in letters have been cut out or scribbled over. As he approached the end of his life, Locke (in Laslett's words) 'took monumental care to face posterity'.

In his will Locke left 'all my manuscripts and all my books that are interleaved, and the one moiety of the rest of my books' to his cousin, Peter King of the Inner Temple, then a young man, later Lord King and direct ancestor of the present Lord Lovelace, from whom the Bodleian in 1947 bought the MSS from Locke's desk and various bound manuscripts as well. The second edition of R. I. Aaron's *John Locke* (1954) contains an appendix on the Lovelace collection. The other moiety of Locke's books remained at High Laver after Locke's death and was known as the Masham moiety. It was dispersed between 1762 and 1916.

The Mellon collection is part of the King moiety; and this gift of manuscripts will eventually be followed by some 800 of Locke's printed books.

Suggestions for Further Reading

EDITIONS OF LOCKE'S WORKS

A complete edition of Locke's works was published in 1714 in 3 vols. by Churchill and Manship, London. Further editions, 1722, 1727, 1740. A 10th edition 1801 in 10 vols.

The most recent edition of the *Thoughts Concerning Education* is by F. W. Garforth, Heinemann, 1964.

There is an edition of the *Essay Concerning Human Understanding* by R. Wilburn, Everyman: Dent, 1947.

LOCKE'S LIFE

Maurice Cranston's *John Locke: a Biography* (Longmans, 1957) is excellent, and includes reference to the Lovelace Collection of MSS, acquired by the Bodleian Library, Oxford, after the Second World War.

LOCKE'S PHILOSOPHY

R. I. Aaron's *John Locke*, O.U.P., 2nd edn, 1955 (1st edn, 1937). The second edition includes an appendix on the Lovelace Collection.

D. J. O'Connor, *John Locke*, Penguin Books, 1952.

GENERAL

The following books will be found helpful for understanding Locke in relation to educational thought before him and after him:

R. H. Quick, *Essays on Educational Reformers*, Longmans. First published 1868, but remains a classic.

J. S. Brubacher, *A History of the Problems of Education*, McGraw-Hill, N.Y., 1947.

S. J. Curtis and M. E. A. Boultwood, *A Short History of Educational Ideas*, University Tutorial Press, 1953.

The Year Book of Education for 1957, *Education and Philosophy*, Evans Bros.

T. L. Jarman, *Landmarks in the History of Education*, John Murray, 1951; 2nd edn, 1963.

G. F. Kneller (ed.), *Foundations of Education*, John Wiley & Sons, Inc., N.Y., 1963.

Index